For Richard + Eleanor

With our love in Christ,
prayers + fond memories
of our pilgrimage to
the Holy Land and
Mount Sinai,

Mother Seraphima
& Sisters

✠

A PILGRIM'S GUIDE

TO THE

HOLY LAND

✠

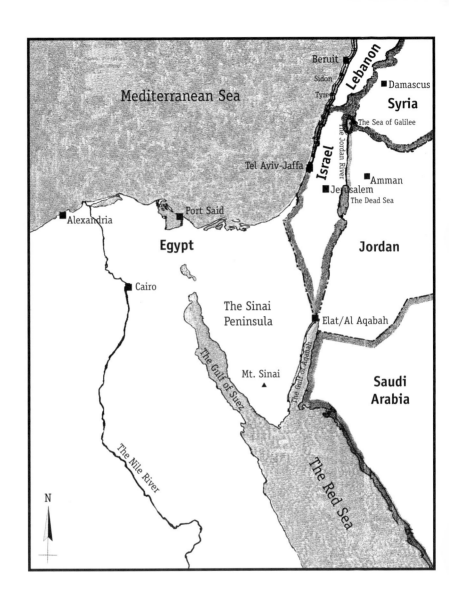

An overview of
The Holy Land & Egypt

A PILGRIM'S GUIDE
TO THE
HOLY LAND

FOR
ORTHODOX CHRISTIANS

by
Holy Nativity Convent

ST. NECTARIOS PRESS
SEATTLE, WASHINGTON

A PILGRIM'S GUIDE TO THE
HOLY LAND
FOR ORTHODOX CHRISTIANS
by
HOLY NATIVITY CONVENT

©1997 Holy Nativity Convent

Scripture Passages are according to the King James Version.

Liturgical Hymns and Psalter Verses ©1974, 1987, 1997 Holy Transfiguration Monastery. Reprinted with permission.

Map on page 154, by Karen S. Westin, is reprinted from MOUNT SINAI by Joseph J. Hobbs, Copyright © 1995. Courtesy of the University of Texas Press.

ISBN: 0-913026-46-8

Library of Congress Number: 97-068989

Published by
ST. NECTARIOS PRESS
10300 ASHWORTH AVENUE NORTH
SEATTLE, WASHINGTON 98133-9410

Typesetting and layout by
Apple Tree Press
Yakima, Washington

Table of Contents

Acknowledgments

With deep gratitude we should like to thank everyone who has assisted us with this publication in any way. Our special thanks to: Reverend Father and Mrs. S. Johnson, E. Dietrich, M. Jerinic, and P. Galarneau.

We should also like to thank those who supplied the many photographs: J. Papson, N. Fotiou, E. Briere, P. Bourdos, A. Diamond, M. Georgeopoulos, E. Bessanova, and Holy Transfiguration Monastery.

St. Nectarios Press would like to express its appreciation to all those who have contributed to this publication financially, and to Gregory Harrison of Apple Tree Press for his tireless efforts in turning the raw material into a finished book.

Prologue

To the Pilgrim:

This little book is not meant to include everything there is to see and do in the Holy Land. It is meant to lead an Orthodox Christian through the major Christian shrines that have been proven by tradition, time, and archaeology to be authentic.

The Orthodox Church has received many things that are not recorded in the Scriptures. A body of knowledge called "tradition" has been passed down from one Orthodox generation to the next. St. Paul speaks of tradition when he says to the Thessalonians, "Stand fast and hold the traditions which ye have received, whether by word or in writing" (II Thess. 2:15). He also relates the tradition he himself had received concerning the Mystical Supper and the Resurrection (I Cor. 11:23; 15:3).

In the Holy Land, in many instances, tradition was the source for both locating the holy sites and explaining their significance. Time and time again, the places and events the Orthodox always held as authentic according to tradition have been proven factual by archaeology or some other science.

The Holy Land is constantly in political turmoil because the territory is claimed by so many religious groups as part of their own traditions. At the shrines that we share, Orthodox pilgrims will often see other religions represented by statues, altars, or pictures. For instance, to the left of the entrance to the Tomb of the Mother of God there is an Armenian altar and tapestries. At Golgotha there is a Latin statue of the Mother of God with a sword in her heart, as well as the Latin altar under the mosaic of the Taking Down from the Cross. The Latins and Protestants each claim a different Shepherds' Field near Bethlehem, but the Orthodox site has been proven to be authentic. A number of sites that cannot be verified by Orthodox tradition have been excluded from this book.

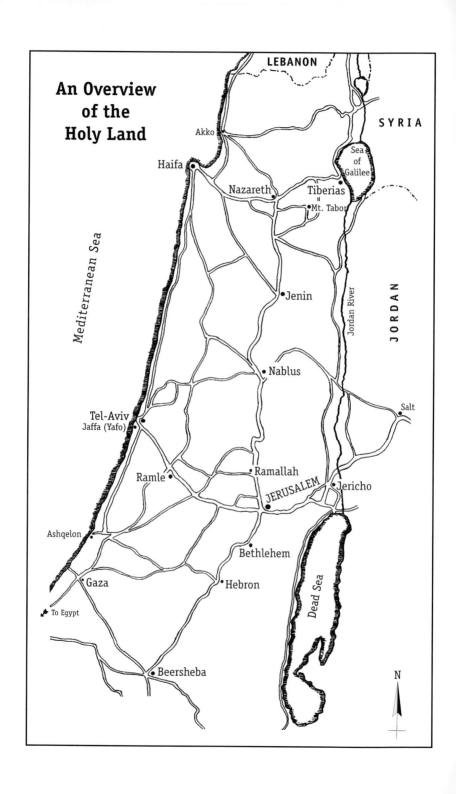

An Overview
of the
Holy Land

Introduction

"Behold, we go up to Jerusalem"
Bridegroom Matins of Holy and Great Monday

Throughout the centuries, multitudes of pilgrims have come to Jerusalem to follow in the footsteps of our Saviour, retracing the paths, the hills, and valleys that He covered during His earthly sojourn which culminated in His Passion, Resurrection, and Ascension. They counted themselves blessed to make any sacrifice: to save the money and other things needed for the journey by denying themselves sometimes even the necessities of life, to travel by foot, by land, or by sea, in order to come even once in their lifetime to venerate the cave in Bethlehem where our Saviour was born, to be immersed in the Jordan River where He was baptized by St. John the Baptist, to bow down at Fearful Golgotha where our Saviour was crucified, and to chant "Christ is Risen" at His Life-Giving Tomb. Many Russian pilgrims who were in Jerusalem for Pascha and received the Holy Fire on Holy Saturday would keep the Fire lit in a lantern and, guarding it carefully, would take it all the way back to their villages in Russia. Not all the pilgrims who travel to Jerusalem today bring back a lantern with the Holy Fire, but they do return with a renewed spiritual strength and zeal and with a heart kindled with a love for the Holy Places sanctified by our Saviour, His All Pure Mother, the Apostles, Prophets, Martyrs, Saints and pious pilgrims throughout the ages. Stephen Graham, author of *With the Russian Pilgrims to Jerusalem* and several other works, wrote, "There is a light on the faces of those living heroically: it is the light of the vision of Jerusalem."[1]

Metropolitan Philaret of Blessed Memory (†1985) often quoted his father, who said that a pilgrimage to Jerusalem is like the fifth gospel, for it makes the other four come to life. Truly, when one is

[1] Steven Graham, *A Tramp's Sketches*, Chapter VI, "The Pilgrimage to Jerusalem," (London: MacMillan & Co., Ltd., 1913), p. 325.

standing at the shrines, at the places where miracles occurred, one feels much closer to the events in the Gospels. And conversely, when one has visited the Holy Land, returns home and reads the Gospels and attends the yearly cycle of the services, one so often returns to the Holy Land in spirit. For example, on the feast of the Nativity of our Saviour when in the Orthros we chant, "Come, ye faithful, let us behold where Christ the Saviour was born," one again descends the steps to see the humble cave where our Saviour "was born of the pure Virgin and Theotokos in Bethlehem of Judea." And on the Glorious Feast of Feasts, the Lord's Pascha, one again feels the joy of standing before the Life-Giving Tomb of our Saviour, where He wrought our salvation in the midst of the earth. On the Sunday of the Samaritan Woman one is again standing in his heart at Jacob's Well and thanking our Saviour for deeming him worthy to drink from the same well; on the Sunday of the Blind Man, one is again transported in his thoughts and heart to the Pool of Siloam...and so follows Feast after Feast.

May this little guide book be of help to today's Holy Land pilgrims, who will follow in our Saviour's footsteps and exclaim as the Apostles did on Mount Tabor, "Yea, Lord, it is good for us to be here."

Transfiguration of our Saviour
August 1997

A
Brief Historical Perspective
of
The Holy Land

At the time of our Saviour, Palestine was a vassal kingdom of the Roman Empire, and Jerusalem was the capital of the province of Judea. Our Saviour was crucified, buried, and arose from the dead outside the city walls of Jerusalem, but by AD 44, the city had expanded so much that these sites were within the city walls. Oppressed by the harshness of Roman rule, the Jews revolted in AD 66. Christian prophets foretold the impending danger, and the Bishop of Jerusalem, a relative of the Saviour, along with many other Christians, relocated to a city beyond the Jordan. The Roman legions sent by Titus to quell the revolt razed the city in 70 AD and then spread salt so that nothing would grow. When the Romans allowed people to return, Jews were not permitted within sight of Jerusalem. Christians were considered to be different from Jews and were permitted to return; thus they were able to preserve the memory of the location of the holy sites. In 135 the Roman Emperor Hadrian levelled the ruins of Jerusalem and built his own city, Aeolia Capitolina. He placed idols on all the holy places of the Christians.

In the 4th century St. Constantine declared Christianity the official religion of the Roman Empire and renamed Palestine "the Holy Land." St. Helen, his mother, brought imperial money and power and built churches over many of the holy sites, creating a place of pilgrimage for all Christians. St. Cyril, Patriarch of Jerusalem (c. 350), greatly developed the liturgical life of the Holy City. As early as 382, the pilgrim Egeria from Spain described a liturgical life in Jerusalem that closely corresponded with the current practices of the Church, especially those for Sundays, Holy Week, and Pascha. The Emperor Justinian (527-565) reorganized, rebuilt, and greatly adorned Jerusalem.

Between 614 and 629 the Persian army, headed by Chosroes, invaded and plundered the Holy Land, martyring several hundred thousand Christians and destroying most of the churches. Greeks were not permitted to remain in the Holy Land, as they were subjects of the Roman Empire and hence distrusted by the Persians. However, Georgia was then a vassal state of the Persian Empire, and since the Persians trusted the Orthodox Georgians, they were permitted to safeguard the shrines at this crucial time.

The Emperor Heraclius wrested the Holy Land from the Persians in 629. He eventually restored the guardianship of the shrines to the Greeks. Shortly afterwards, in 640, the Holy Land was besieged and taken under Moslem Arab rule. The Arabs systematically persecuted all non-Moslems in the Holy Land in the mid-8th century. Christians were constrained to convert to Islam, to flee, or to become crypto-Christians, hiding their true belief under the externals of Moslem worship. These persecutions forced the abandonment of monasteries, churches and shrines, many of which were taken over by Moslems, while others fell into ruins.

In the late 11th century, after the schism between the Orthodox and the Church of Rome, a Latin hermit named Peter traversed the European countryside preaching about the desecration of the holy places and inspiring Latins to rise up against the oppression of the Christians in the Holy Land. The Pope of Rome, seeing the fervor for war that Peter had created among the landowners, used this opportunity to further his own goals. He granted indulgences to those who would go to war to gain the Holy Land for the Latin Church. This occupied the young warriors, thus terminating the feudal skirmishes that had been rampant. With "spiritual" as well as material motives, noblemen from Western Europe banded together in 1095 and invaded the Holy Land in several Crusades. They succeeded in driving out the Moslems in 1099. Once established, the Latin Crusaders persecuted Moslems and even other Christians, forcing the Orthodox in Jerusalem to remain in hiding. The Latin Kingdom survived until the Crusaders were defeated and evicted in 1187 by the Egyptian Moslem Mamelukes. The rule of the Mamelukes was noted for its brutality, destruction, and the misery of the conquered, which then led to a general decline in the Holy Land.

Three hundred and thirty years later, in 1517, the Ottoman Turks, having conquered the Byzantine Empire, turned their army against the weaker Mamelukes and gained possession of the Holy Land. No significant changes occurred to ease the oppression and sufferings of the local Christian population, which was Orthodox except for the Monophysite Armenian colony. The Ottoman Empire granted favors to the Armenians and Franciscans in the Holy Land in exchange for large sums of money. Intense rivalries between the Orthodox, Franciscans, and Armenians over the guardianship of the holy places served as a cause of the Crimean War, 1853-1856. In 1856, the *Status Quo* was drafted. Still in effect, this document enumerates the holdings and rights of each religious group, and sets guidelines for the common use of certain shrines.

In the late 19th century, the Zionist movement encouraged European Jews to move to the Holy Land. The *Balfour Declaration* of 1917, supporting a "Jewish home in Palestine," stimulated increased Jewish immigration after World War I. The Palestinians under the British Mandate initially welcomed these immigrants. However, after World War II, large numbers of socialist Jews settled in Palestine. Their more radical elements began a campaign of terror against the British authorities and the Palestinian people, leading to the withdrawal of the British and the proclamation of the secular Zionist state of Israel in 1948. A civil war immediately erupted, ending in an armistice in 1949, which divided Jerusalem between Israel and Jordan. After the Six Day War in 1967, Israel extended its control to the rest of Jerusalem and most of the territory which in Biblical times had belonged to the twelve tribes of Israel. The Palestinians, many of whom are Christians, remain unreconciled to the loss of the land that had been their home for over a thousand years, and conflicts between them and the Jews have remained common up to the present time.

The Old City
of
Jerusalem

I was glad because of them that said unto me: Let us go into the
house of the Lord. Our feet have stood in thy courts,
O Jerusalem. (Ps. 121:1-2)

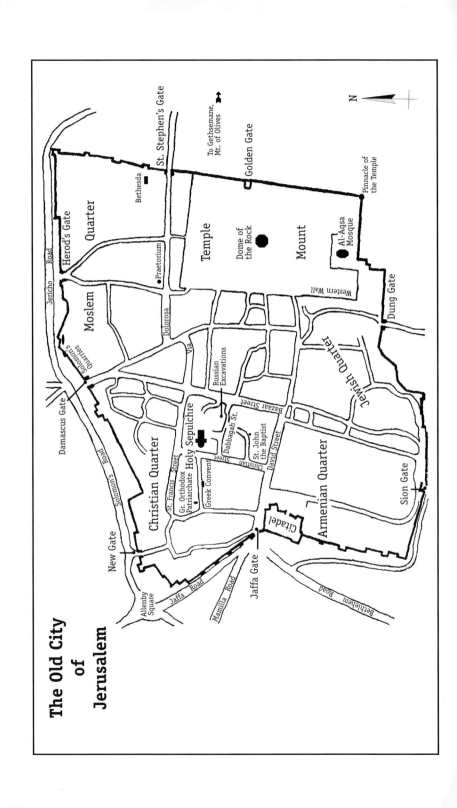

Jerusalem

The pilgrim's first view of the Old City of Jerusalem is of its strong walls, last rebuilt in the 16th century by Suleiman the Magnificent along the boundaries of the Roman city. There are eight gates in the walls of Jerusalem today. Two of them are walled up, and several are not designed for defense, as they were built in a time of peace. The city's main entrance, the **Damascus Gate** (so named because it is the beginning of the road to Damascus), is located on the north side. This gate was well organized for defense with arrow slits (some now widened for easier access with guns), holes for pouring boiling oil, and a protected walkway for guards. Within the gate itself, the road makes several sharp turns which prevent invaders from entering the city suddenly. The causeway which leads to the gate was built in 1966-67 to span an archaeological dig which has uncovered a Roman gate from AD 135.

The Damascus Gate on the north side of the Old City of Jerusalem. Street vendors often line the route to the entrance.

In the 6th century, the Emperor Justinian built the Cardo Maximus, a street seventy feet (21m) wide beginning at the Damascus Gate and crossing the entire city. Some of the pillars which lined this avenue have been found in excavations in the store basements along the ancient street. A portion of the Cardo Maximus has been restored and is used as a subterranean shopping area near the Jewish Quarter.

The 6th century Madaba mosaic map shows with surprising detail the Cardo Maximus, the Church of the Holy Sepulchre, the Damascus Gate, and approximately 150 other identifiable structures. The original map was located in a church in the small village of Madaba, east of the Dead Sea. It was discovered c. 1890 when it was almost destroyed during the rebuilding of the church. A replica of the Madaba Map is located in the YMCA in New Jerusalem.

In addition to its shrines, the Old City is home to thousands of Orthodox Christians, Jews, Moslems, and Armenians, each group living in its own neighborhood (or "quarter") in a somewhat uneasy co-existence with the others. The city is oriental in character; many of the steep, narrow streets are lined with open shops, and vendors compete for attention and business. Residences are built or grouped around courtyards with gates which open into the street and are closed at night. In the Christian Quarter, several vacant monasteries have been converted into apartments.

The Holy Sepulchre Complex

The heart of Christendom and ultimate goal of all Christian pilgrims, the Holy Sepulchre Complex lies nestled in the center of the Christian quarter. A small, arched doorway in Dabbagah Street has a modest sign beside it, stating simply: Holy Sepulchre. Passing through the archway, the pilgrim finds himself in the large cobblestone courtyard of the Holy Sepulchre Complex. The original church built by St. Constantine in 325-335 was approximately twice the size

The Holy Sepulchre Complex as seen from the roof of an adjacent building.

of the present building and was regally adorned with gold, silver, many different colors of marble, and numerous mosaics. This church was ravaged by the invading Persians in 614 and has never regained its original splendor. It has been rebuilt or repaired countless times because of damage caused by invaders, zealous Moslems, and earthquakes. Most of the present architectural style is the work of the Crusaders who rebuilt the church during their residence. Over the centuries, the necessary repairs have not been carried out systematically, and the church is an architectural medley. It is now shared by

9

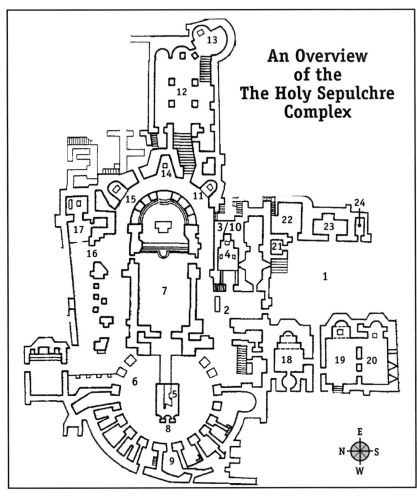

An Overview of the The Holy Sepulchre Complex

Legend

1. The Courtyard
2. The Anointing Stone
3. Holy Golgotha
4. Adam's Chapel
5. The Kouvouklion
6. The Rotunda
7. The Catholicon
8. A Coptic Chapel
9. Chapel of the Syrians
10. Chapel of the Sacrifice of Abraham (above Holy Golgotha)
11. Chapel of the Crowning
12. Chapel of St. Helen
13. Crypt of the Finding of the True Cross
14. Chapel of the Sharing of the Raiment
15. Chapel of St. Longinus
16. Chapel of the Clappes
17. Temporary Prison
18. Church of the Forty Martyrs of Sebastia
19. Church of the Myrrh-Bearing Women
20. Church of St. James
21. Chapel of St. Mary of Egypt
22. Chapel of the Copts
23. Chapel of the Armenians
24. Entrance into the Convent of Abraham

the Orthodox, Armenians, Latins, Syrians, Copts, and a small Ethiopian Christian monastery located on the roof.

Originally, the entrance to the church was a double doorway, of which the eastern door is now blocked up. To the left of the western door on the outside are three marble pillars, the middle one having a large crack in it. In 1580 the Armenians were intrigued by the Holy Fire that miraculously issues from the Tomb of our Saviour each year on Holy Saturday. They bribed the Moslem rulers to lock

The cracked pillar from which the Holy Fire came in 1580, when the Orthodox Christians were locked out of the Holy Sepulchre.

the Orthodox out of the church on that day, thinking to receive and keep the Holy Fire for themselves. The Orthodox remained praying in the courtyard, hoping that the Armenians would share the Fire with them when it appeared. The usual time of the Fire's arrival passed and all began to pray more fervently. Suddenly, the pillar cracked and the Holy Fire issued from the crack, bringing much joy to the Orthodox while shaming the Armenians in the church.

11

One of the Moslem soldiers on duty on the minaret at the back corner of the courtyard (the El-Omariyeh Mosque) saw the Holy Fire issuing from the pillar. In that instant he believed. "Great is the God of the Christians!" he exclaimed, and leaped from the minaret. When he landed in the courtyard below, he left footprints in the stone, as if the pavement had been soft wax. Moslem soldiers below killed him instantly for his confession of the Orthodox Faith. His footprints, which proclaimed the miracle, were also eradicated by the Moslems. The Orthodox Church celebrates the memory of St. Tounom on April 10/23.

THE ANOINTING STONE

St. Mark 15:43-47

At that time, Joseph of Arimathæa, an honourable counsellor, which also waited for the Kingdom of God, came, and went in boldly unto Pilate, and craved the body of Jesus. And Pilate marvelled if He were already dead: and calling unto him the centurion, he asked him whether He had been any while dead. And when he knew it of the centurion, he gave the body to Joseph. And he bought fine linen, and took Him down, and wrapped Him in the linen, and laid Him in a sepulchre which was hewn out of a rock, and rolled a stone unto the door of the sepulchre. And Mary Magdalene and Mary the mother of Joses beheld where He was laid.

Directly ahead upon entering the church one finds the Anointing Stone, which marks the location where the Lord's Body was laid when He was being prepared for burial by Nicodemus and Joseph. Inscribed on the stone is the dismissal troparion (in its shorter

The Anointing Stone marks the place where St. Joseph of Arimathaea "took down the body of Jesus and wound it in linen clothes with the spices, as the manner of the Jews to is bury" (John 19:40). As one faces the Anointing Stone with his back to the door, to the right are the stairs to Golgotha and to the left is the passageway to the Rotunda and the Tomb of our Lord and God and Saviour Jesus Christ.

form), which is chanted at Vespers on Holy and Great Friday and on the Sunday of the Myrrh-Bearing Women, and recited by the priest as he lays the Holy Gifts upon the Holy Table at the Divine Liturgy.

✠

Dismissal Troparion of the Sunday of the Myrrh-Bearing Women
Second Tone

The noble Joseph, taking Thine immaculate Body down from the Tree, and having wrapped It in pure linen and spices, laid It for burial in a new tomb. But on the third day Thou didst arise, O Lord, granting great mercy to the world.

✠

On the right, immediately after passing the Anointing Stone, is a very steep, narrow staircase. This leads to Golgotha.

GOLGOTHA

(St. Matthew 27:27-56; St. Mark 15:21-41; St. Luke 23:26-49; St. John 19:16-37)

St. Matthew 27:27-56

And it came to pass that the soldiers of the governor took Jesus into the common hall, and gathered unto Him the whole band of soldiers. And they stripped Him, and put on Him a scarlet robe. And when they had platted a crown of thorns, they put it upon His head, and a reed in His right hand: and they bowed the knee before Him, and mocked Him, saying, Hail, King of the Jews! And they spit upon Him, and took the reed, and smote Him on the head. And after that they had mocked Him, they took the robe off from Him, and put His own raiment on Him, and led Him away to crucify Him. And as they came out, they found a man of Cyrene, Simon by name: him they compelled to bear His cross. And when they were come unto a place called Golgotha, that is to say, a Place of a Skull, they gave Him vinegar to drink mingled with gall: and when He had tasted thereof, He would not drink. And they crucified Him, and parted His garments, casting lots: that it might be fulfilled which was spoken by the Prophet, They parted My garments among them, and upon

My vesture did they cast lots. And sitting down they watched Him there; and set up over His head His accusation written, THIS IS JESUS THE KING OF THE JEWS. Then were there two thieves crucified with Him, one on the right hand, and another on the left. And they that passed by reviled Him, wagging their heads, and saying, Thou that destroyest the temple, and buildest it in three days, save Thyself. If Thou be the Son of God, come down from the cross. Likewise also the chief priests mocking Him, with the scribes and elders, said, He saved others; Himself He cannot save. If He be the King of Israel, let Him now come down from the cross, and we will believe Him. He trusted in God; let Him deliver Him now, if He will have Him: for He said, I am the Son of God. The thieves also, which were crucified with Him, cast the same in His teeth. Now from the sixth hour there was darkness over all the land unto the ninth hour. And about the ninth hour Jesus cried with a loud voice, saying, Eli, Eli, lama sabachthani? that is to say, My God, My God, why hast Thou forsaken Me? Some of them that stood there, when they heard that, said, This man calleth for Elias. And straightway one of them ran, and took a spunge, and filled it with vinegar, and put it on a reed, and gave Him to drink. The rest said, Let be, let us see whether Elias will come to save Him. Jesus, when He had cried again with a loud voice, yielded up the spirit. And, behold, the veil of the temple was rent in twain from the top to the bottom; and the earth did quake, and the rocks rent; and the graves were opened; and many bodies of the Saints which slept arose, and came out of the graves after His resurrection, and went into the holy city, and appeared unto many. Now when the centurion, and they that were with him, watching Jesus, saw the earthquake, and those things that were done, they feared greatly, saying, Truly this was the Son of God. And many women were there beholding afar off, which followed Jesus from Galilee, ministering unto Him: among which was Mary Magdalene, and Mary the mother of James and Joses, and the mother of Zebedee's children.

When the Persians ravaged the Holy Land in 614, they carried off the Precious Cross as a trophy. Fourteen years later, the Emperor Heraclius defeated the Persians and brought the Cross back to Jerusalem amidst much rejoicing and pomp. When he reached the level of Golgotha, the crown fell from his head. Our Lord Jesus Christ, the King of Glory, reigns here and, regardless of rank, no one is permitted to wear a crown or miter on Golgotha.

A life-sized icon of our Lord on the Cross with the Mother of God and St. John standing sorrowfully below adorns this place. Behind them are icons with silver rizas of scenes from His Passion. Under the Holy Table is an icon and a silver disc. Through the hole in the center of the disc one can touch the rounded stone covering the spot where the Cross of our Lord stood. To protect it, the mountain of Golgotha had been encased in marble; now it is covered in plexiglass. To the right of the row of pillars is the Roman Catholic chapel of the Taking Down from the Cross.

Holy Golgotha. The place where the Saviour's Cross stood can be touched under the Holy Table.

After descending the same staircase, to the right is a passageway which leads to **Adam's Chapel**. On the far side of the chapel, beyond the iron grate, one can see a window which frames the crack in the rock of Golgotha that was made when the earth quaked at the time of the Crucifixion. Orthodox tradition teaches that our Lord, the new Adam, was crucified on the very spot where the skull of the first man, Adam, was buried. The blood of our

Saviour dripped from the Cross onto the skull of Adam, thereby redeeming all of mankind from the state of sin. Many Orthodox icons depict Adam's skull under the Cross of our Lord.

✠

Theotokion of the Cross
First Tone

On seeing Thine unjust slaughter, O Christ, the pure Virgin cried in grief, "O most sweet Child, how is it that Thou diest lawlessly? How is it that Thou Who hast suspended all the earth upon the floods of waters art now Thyself suspended from the Tree? O most merciful Benefactor, do not leave me, Thy Mother and Handmaid alone."

✠

THE LIFE-GIVING TOMB

(St. Matthew 27:57-28:8; St. Mark 15:42-16:8; St. Luke 23:50-24:12; St. John 19:38-20:10)

St. Mark 15:42-16:8

When the even was come, because it was the preparation, that is, the day before the sabbath, Joseph of Arimathæa, an honourable counsellor, which also waited for the Kingdom of God, came, and went in boldly unto Pilate, and craved the body of Jesus. And Pilate marvelled if He had been any while dead. And when he knew it of the centurion, he gave the body to Joseph. And he bought fine linen, and took Him down, and wrapped Him in the linen, and laid Him in a sepulchre which was hewn out of a rock, and rolled a stone unto the door of the sepulchre. And Mary Magdalene and Mary the mother of Joses beheld where He was laid. And when the sabbath was past, Mary Magdalene, and Mary the mother of James, and Salome, had bought sweet spices, that they might come and anoint Him. And very early in the morning the first day of the week, they came unto the sepulchre at the rising of the sun. And they said among themselves, Who shall roll us away the stone from the door of the sepulchre? And when they looked, they saw that the stone was rolled away: for it was very great. And entering into the sepulchre, they saw a young man sitting on the right side, clothed in a long white garment; and they were affrighted. And he saith unto them, Be not affrighted: Ye seek Jesus of

Nazareth, which was crucified: He is risen; He is not here: behold the place where they laid Him. But go your way, tell His disciples and Peter that He goeth before you into Galilee: there shall ye see Him, as He said unto you. And they went out quickly, and fled from the sepulchre; for they trembled and were amazed: neither said they any thing to any man; for they were afraid.

The Kouvouklion containing the life-bearing Tomb of our Lord and God and Saviour Jesus Christ was built in 1801. Through the first doorway is the Angel's Chapel.

☩

Hymn from the Paschal Hours

How life-giving, how much more beautiful than paradise, and truly more resplendent than any royal palace proved Thy grave, the source of our resurrection, O Christ.

☩

To the left of the Anointing Stone is a passageway leading to the Rotunda, the circular area under the main dome of the Holy Sepulchre Complex, and the Tomb of our Lord and God and Saviour Jesus Christ. The Tomb is enclosed within a highly ornamented marble building called the **Kouvouklion**. Excavations made under the Tomb have verified the tradition that the area was first a quarry, then a cemetery, and then a garden. Over the entrance are three sets of oil lamps burning before three icons of our Saviour: one set for the Orthodox, one for the Armenians, and one for the Latins, the three groups that have permission to serve in the Tomb. The Copts do not have permission to use the Tomb for any of their services so they have a small chapel attached to the back of the Kouvouklion.

The exterior of the Kouvouklion has many Greek inscriptions, most of which are Scriptural passages about our Lord's Burial and Resurrection. Through the first doorway is the **Angel's Chapel**. Encased in the marble vessel in the center of the room is the remainder of the stone that was rolled away from the door of the Tomb. The

Interior of the Tomb of our Lord. The place where our Lord's Body was laid.

inscription reads, *"For the Angel of the Lord descended and rolled back the stone from the door"* (St. Matthew 28:2). Two openings on either side of the chapel are used by the Patriarch on Holy Saturday for distributing the Holy Fire.

The Tomb itself is reached through the second doorway, which is so low that one must enter bowing. Only four or five people can fit inside at the same time. The actual stone on which our Lord's Body was laid has been encased in marble. To the left of the stone is an icon of the Mother of God. Behind this is a portion of the original wall of the Tomb. In order to show reverence, Orthodox pilgrims do not turn their backs to the Tomb when leaving; they exit walking backwards.

✠

Dismissal Troparion of Pascha
First Tone
Christ is risen from the dead, by death hath He trampled down death, and on those in the graves hath He bestowed life.

✠

Opposite the entrance to the Kouvouklion is the main church of the Holy Sepulchre Complex, the **Catholicon**, which is dedicated to the Resurrection of Christ. Because "He hath wrought salvation in the midst of the earth" (Psalm 73:13), in the middle of the Catholicon is the "Navel of the world," a carved urn-shaped object depicting the center of the world.

Across from the Coptic chapel behind the Kouvouklion is the Chapel of the Syrians. Located here are several tombs from the time of our Saviour which may be the tombs of Joseph and Nicodemus, but this theory has not been verified. Regardless, they are good examples of what tombs were like in those days — narrow and carved out of the solid rock. The deceased was wrapped in a shroud and slid into the tomb; a rock was then rolled to cover the opening. The tomb would be opened when the next family member died.

*The Catholicon of the Holy Sepulchre Complex,
the Church of the Resurrection.*

✠

Kontakion of the Dedication of the Church of the Holy Resurrection
Fourth Tone
to "On this day Thou hast appeared"

The Church is shown to be a many-lighted heaven that doth shine a
guiding light upon all them that do believe; wherein, while standing
we cry aloud: Do Thou Thyself now establish this house, O Lord.

✠

OTHER CHAPELS IN THE HOLY SEPULCHRE COMPLEX

Directly above Golgotha is a small chapel twelve feet square, dedicated to the Sacrifice of Abraham. The Church teaches that the sacrificing of Isaac was a foreshadowing of our Saviour's sacrifice. Therefore, the same mountain served as a place of burial for Adam, the place of Abraham's sacrifice, and the Crucifixion of our Lord. This chapel was given to the Anglicans during the British Mandate Government.

The right side of the wide corridor that goes completely around the Catholicon is lined with chapels commemorating different people and events related to the Passion of our Saviour. To the right of Adam's Chapel is the **Chapel of the Crowning with Thorns (Oratory of the Insults)** which contains a portion of a granite column. Some sources state that our Saviour was bound to this column when the soldiers mocked and scourged Him.

After this chapel a stone stairway leads down to the Armenian Chapel of St. Helen. In their joy, pilgrims through the centuries have carved crosses and other inscriptions into the walls. Continuing down the second flight of stairs on the right, one enters the **Crypt of the Finding of the True Cross.** In ancient times, this area was a cistern and in the time of our Lord it was used as a garbage dump. When St. Helen began her search for the True Cross, one of the local inhabitants remembered where the Cross of our Lord was buried and directed St. Helen to dig in that area. On the left as the pilgrim descends the stairs is a window commemorating the spot where St. Helen stood throwing coins to the workers, urging them to dig faster in her eagerness to reach the Invincible Trophy.

At the place marked by the marble slab on the ground, three crosses were found. The inscription by Pilate was also found, but it was separate from the Cross. The Patriarch of Jerusalem at that time, St. Macarius, took the crosses to the bedside of a dying patrician woman and laid them, one at a time, upon her. When the Precious Cross touched her, she immediately opened her eyes, regained her strength, and was able to rise from her bed. In the same manner a dead man was restored to life.

The Crypt of the Finding of the True Cross. The place where the Precious and Life-Giving Cross was found is marked by an iron railing and inlaid marble slab.

✠

Dismissal Troparion of the Cross
First Tone

Save, O Lord, Thy people and bless Thine inheritance; grant Thou unto the faithful victory over adversaries. And by the power of Thy Cross, do Thou preserve Thy commonwealth.

✠

Continuing counterclockwise around the Catholicon, the next chapel is the **Chapel of the Sharing of the Raiment**, which commemorates the soldiers parting the raiment of our Saviour and casting lots for His vesture (St. John 19:24). Next is the **Chapel of St. Longinus the Centurion**. A Cappadocian by birth, he was a Centurion in the Roman army stationed in Jerusalem. As a witness of the Crucifixion, he said, "Truly this was the Son of God" (St. Matthew 27:54). He was also on guard at the Tomb at the time of the Resurrection. He believed and was baptized, then fled to his homeland because the Jews sought to kill him for his confession of the truth. There he converted many to the Faith, but the Jews, learning of his labors in preaching, had him beheaded.

Northwest of the Chapel of St. Longinus is an area called the **Chapel of the Clappes**. It commemorates the soldiers putting Christ's feet in a clamp. Directly behind and to the left of this area is an example of a temporary prison, like the one which would have held our Lord while the soldiers made the necessary preparations.

Depending on the day and time, pilgrims might be permitted to enter some of the chapels that ring the courtyard. On the left side of the courtyard as one faces the entrance are chapels dedicated to the Forty Martyrs of Sebastia, the Myrrh-Bearing Women, and St. James the Brother of the Lord. Under the stairs to the right of the main entrance to the church is the Chapel of St. Mary of Egypt. Along the right wall is the Chapel of the Copts, the Chapel of the Armenians, and the entrance to the Convent of Abraham.

Other Sites in the Old City

RUSSIAN EXCAVATIONS

St. Luke 23:1-34

At that time, the whole multitude of them arose, and led Him unto Pilate. And they began to accuse Him, saying, We found this fellow perverting the nation, and forbidding to give tribute to Cæsar, saying that He Himself is Christ a King. And Pilate asked Him, saying, Art Thou the King of the Jews? And He answered him and said, Thou sayest it. Then said Pilate to the chief priests and to the people, I find no fault in this man. And they were the more fierce, saying, He stirreth up the people, teaching throughout all Jewry, beginning from Galilee to this place. When Pilate heard of Galilee, he asked whether the man were a Galilæan. And as soon as he knew that He belonged unto Herod's jurisdiction, he sent Him to Herod, who himself also was at Jerusalem at that time. And when Herod saw Jesus, he was exceeding glad: for he was desirous to see Him of a long season, because he had heard many things of Him; and he hoped to have seen some miracle done by Him. Then he questioned with Him in many words; but He answered him nothing. And the chief priests and scribes stood and vehemently accused Him. And Herod with his men of war set Him at nought, and mocked Him, and arrayed Him in a gorgeous robe, and sent Him again to Pilate. And the same day Pilate and Herod were made friends together: for before they were at enmity between themselves. And Pilate, when he had called together the chief priests and the rulers and the people, said unto them, Ye have brought this man unto me, as one that perverteth the people: and, behold, I, having examined Him before you, have found no fault in this man touching those things whereof ye accuse Him: No, nor yet Herod: for I sent you to him; and, lo, nothing worthy of death is found in Him. I will therefore chastise Him, and release Him. (For of necessity he must release one unto them at the feast.) And they cried out all at once, saying, Away with this man, and release unto us Barabbas (who for a certain sedition made in the city, and for murder, was cast into prison.) Pilate therefore, willing to release Jesus, spake again to them. But they cried, saying, Crucify Him, crucify Him. And he said unto them the third time, Why, what evil hath He done? I have found no cause of death in Him: I will therefore chastise Him, and let Him go. And they were instant with loud voices, requiring that He might be crucified. And the voices of them and of the chief priests prevailed. And Pilate gave sentence that it should be as they required. And he released unto them him that for sedition and murder was cast into prison, whom they had desired; but he delivered Jesus to their will. And as they led Him away, they laid hold upon one Simon, a Cyrenian, coming out of the country, and on him they laid the cross, that he might bear it after Jesus. And there followed Him a great company of people, and of women, which also bewailed and lamented Him. But Jesus turning unto them said, Daughters of Jerusalem, weep not for Me, but weep for yourselves, and for your children. For, behold, the days are coming, in the which they shall say, Blessed are the barren, and the wombs that never bare, and the paps which never gave suck. Then shall they begin to say to the mountains, Fall on us; and to the hills, Cover us. For if they do these things in a green tree, what shall be done in the dry? And there were also two other, malefactors, led with Him to be put to death. And when they were come to the place, which is called Calvary, there they crucified Him, and the malefactors, one on the right hand, and the other on the left. Then said Jesus, Father, forgive them; for they know not what they do. And they parted His raiment, and cast lots.

The Russian Excavations, also known as the **Church of St. Alexander Nevsky**, is located a short distance from the Holy Sepulchre, at 25 Dabbagah Street. During the latter half of the last century there were many Russian pilgrims to the Holy Land. This property was purchased to build a hostel for the upper class Russian pilgrims. While excavating for the foundation, the pillars that had lined Justinian's main street, the Cardo Maximus, were found. Further excavations uncovered a segment of the Herodian city wall, which proved that the Tomb had indeed been outside the city. Of particular significance was the discovery of the threshold and the holes for the posts of the Judgment Gate, the gate through which our Saviour was led to crucifixion. According to Jewish law, any man could wait at that gate for the condemned and could demand a retrial if there was any new evidence, but no one spoke up for our Saviour.

St. Constantine's church of the Holy Sepulchre was so large that it included the Judgment Gate area. In the Church of St. Alexander there is a Holy Table carved out of solid rock, which was originally from the chapel that St. Constantine built over the area. A room off the church houses a small museum that contains nails from New Testament times, metal crosses and weights worn by Russian pilgrims on their way to Jerusalem, a scale model of the main dome of the Holy Sepulchre, and other items of interest.

The **Praetorium,** a typical example of prisons during the time of our Saviour, is located in a Greek Orthodox Monastery on the Via Dolorosa. One must use caution climbing down the smooth stone

The Judgment Gate, found in the Russian Excavations. The case on the floor surrounded by oil lamps protects the threshold and holes from the posts of the gate our Saviour passed through on His way to crucifixion.

stairs, as they are slightly damp and very slippery. Prisoners cast into these deep, ancient caves cut out of rock had no escape unless a rope were lowered and they were pulled out. A section with smaller, deeper chambers was generally reserved for the condemned.

BETHESDA

At that time, Jesus went up to Jerusalem. Now there is at Jerusalem by the sheep market a pool, which is called in the Hebrew tongue Bethesda, having five porches. In these lay a great multitude of impotent folk, of blind, halt, withered, waiting for the moving of the water. For an Angel went down at a certain season into the pool, and troubled the water: whosoever then first after the troubling of the water stepped in was made whole of whatsoever disease he had. And a certain man was there, which had an infirmity thirty and eight years. When Jesus saw him lie, and knew that he had been now a long time in that case, He saith unto him, Wilt thou be made whole? The impotent man answered Him, Sir, I have no man, when the water is troubled, to put me into the pool: but while I am coming, another steppeth down before me. Jesus saith unto him, Rise, take up thy bed, and walk. And immediately the man was made whole, and took up his bed, and walked: and on the same day was the sabbath. The Jews therefore said unto him that was cured, It is the sabbath day: it is not lawful for thee to carry thy bed. He answered them, He that made me whole, the same said unto me, Take up thy bed, and walk. Then asked they him, What man is that which said unto thee, Take up thy bed, and walk? And he that was healed wist not who it was: for Jesus had conveyed Himself away, a multitude being in that place. Afterward Jesus findeth him in the temple, and said unto him, Behold, thou art made whole: sin no more, lest a worse thing come unto thee. The man departed, and told the Jews that it was Jesus, which had made him whole.

Bethesda, also known as the **Sheep's Pool**, is the place where, from Hebrew times, sheep that were to be sacrificed in the Temple were washed. Here the paralytic lay for thirty-eight years waiting to be healed at the moving of the waters, until our Saviour came and healed him. Through the centuries many churches have been built on this site, and extensive excavations have located several different levels of ruins, as well as the tombstone of the deacon, Amos, who was attached to one of the churches on the site. This tombstone inscribed in Greek, the first solid evidence that the site is indeed Bethesda, can be seen opposite the Crusader church of St. Anne. There are signs directing one's attention to interesting aspects of the excavations. It is advised that pilgrims do not go down to the water as the staircase is very worn and the water is now contaminated. The borders of the flower beds by the entrance contain many carved stone artifacts found in the excavations.

Bethesda, "The Sheep's Pool," where the Saviour healed the paralytic. The Church commemorates this miracle on the 3rd Sunday after Pascha.

✠

Kontakion for the Sunday of the Paralytic
Third Tone
to "On this day the Virgin"

As of old Thou didst raise up the paralytic, O Lord God, by Thy God-like care and might, raise up my soul which is palsied by diverse sins and transgressions and by unseemly deeds and acts, that, saved, I may also cry out: O Compassionate Redeemer, O Christ God, glory to Thy dominion and might.

✠

The Environs
of
Jerusalem

They that trust in the Lord shall be as Mount Sion;
he that dwelleth at Jerusalem, nevermore shall he be shaken.
(Ps. 124:1)

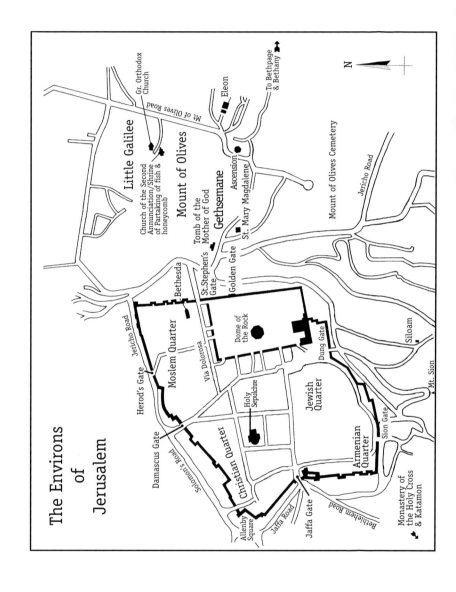

The Environs of Jerusalem

Little Galilee
Church of the Second Annunciation/Shrine of Partaking of fish & honeycomb
Gr. Orthodox Church
Mt of Olives Road
Eleon
To Bethpage & Bethany
Mount of Olives
Tomb of the Mother of God
Gethsemane
Ascension
St. Mary Magdalene
Mount of Olives Cemetery
Jericho Road
St.Stephen's Gate
Golden Gate
Bethesda
Moslem Quarter
Via Dolorosa
Herod's Gate
Jericho Road
Dome of the Rock
Damascus Gate
Solomon's Road
Holy Sepulchre
Christian Quarter
Dung Gate
Siloam
Jewish Quarter
Mt. Sion
Armenian Quarter
Sion Gate
Allenby Square
Jaffa Road
Jaffa Gate
Bethlehem Road
Monastery of the Holy Cross & Katamon

N

Siloam

St. John 9:1-38

At that time, as Jesus passed by, He saw a man which was blind from his birth. And His disciples asked Him, saying, Master, who did sin, this man, or his parents, that he was born blind? Jesus answered, Neither hath this man sinned, nor his parents: but that the works of God should be made manifest in him. I must work the works of Him that sent Me, while it is day: the night cometh, when no man can work. As long as I am in the world, I am the light of the world. When He had thus spoken, He spat on the ground, and made clay of the spittle, and He anointed the eyes of the blind man with the clay, and said unto him, Go, wash in the pool of Siloam, (which is by interpretation, Sent.) He went his way therefore, and washed, and came seeing. The neighbours therefore, and they which before had seen him that he was blind, said, Is not this he that sat and begged? Some said, This is he: others said, He is like him: but he said, I am he. Therefore said they unto him, How were thine eyes opened? He answered and said, A man that is called Jesus made clay, and anointed mine eyes, and said unto me, Go to the pool of Siloam, and wash: and I went and washed, and I received sight. Then said they unto him, Where is He? He said, I know not. They brought to the Pharisees him that aforetime was blind. And it was the sabbath day when Jesus made the clay, and opened his eyes. Then again the Pharisees also asked him how he had received his sight. He said unto them, He put clay upon mine eyes, and I washed, and do see. Therefore said some of the Pharisees, This man is not of God, because He keepeth not the sabbath day. Others said, How can a man that is a sinner do such miracles? And there was a division among them. They say unto the blind man again, What sayest thou of Him, that He hath opened thine eyes? He said, He is a Prophet. But the Jews did not believe concerning him, that he had been blind, and received his sight, until they called the parents of him that had received his sight. And they asked them, saying, Is this your son, who ye say was born blind? How then doth he now see? His parents answered them and said, We know that this is our son, and that he was born blind: but by what means he now seeth, we know not; or who hath opened his eyes, we know not: he is of age; ask him: he shall speak for himself. These words spake his parents, because they feared the Jews: for the Jews had agreed already, that if any man did confess that He was the Christ, he should be put out of the synagogue. Therefore said his parents, He is of age; ask him. Then again called they the man that was blind, and said unto him, Give God the praise: we know that this man is a sinner. He answered and said, Whether He be a sinner or no, I know not: one thing I know, that, whereas I was blind, now I see. Then said they to him again, What did He to thee? how opened He thine eyes? He answered them, I have told you already, and ye did not hear: wherefore would ye hear it again? will ye also be His disciples? Then they reviled him, and said, Thou art His disciple; but we are Moses' disciples. We know that God spake unto Moses: as for this fellow, we know not from whence He is. The man answered and said unto them, Why herein is a marvellous thing, that ye know not from whence He is, and yet He hath opened mine eyes. Now we know that God heareth not sinners: but if any man be a worshipper of God, and doeth His will, him He heareth. Since the world began was it not heard that any man opened the eyes of one that was born blind. If this man were not of God, He could do nothing. They answered and said unto him, Thou wast altogether born in sins, and dost thou teach us? And they cast him out. Jesus heard that they had cast him out; and when He had found him, He said unto him, Dost thou believe on the Son of God? He answered and said, Who is He, Lord, that I might believe on Him? And Jesus said unto him, Thou hast both seen Him, and it is He that talketh with thee. And he said, Lord, I believe. And he worshipped Him.

When the Prophet Esaias was being sawn in half with a wooden saw by the Jews outside Jerusalem, God heard his request for water to quench his thirst and the Spring Gihon gushed forth. This spring served as the main source of fresh water to the city for many centuries. To avoid being cut off from this important source of water during a siege of the city, in 701 BC King Hezekiah had a tunnel carved through the rock from both ends by two work crews, creating the pool of Siloam inside the city. At the point where the two crews met, there was an inscription in the rock describing this remarkable architectural feat.

At the time of the Gospel narrative, our Saviour had been speaking in the Temple but the Jews would not accept His teachings. He withdrew from them and proved His words by healing the blind man. The holy Fathers of the Church say that this miracle was especially incredible to the Jews because the man was not just born blind, he was born without eyes. In anointing his eyes, our Saviour – He Who took the dust of the earth and made man – fashioned eyes for him.

Pool of Siloam, where the Saviour sent the man blind from birth, commemorated on the 5th Sunday after Pascha. The end of King Hezekiah's Tunnel can be seen in the far wall under the arch.

Siloam means "sent" and it was to this spring, which was not then known for its curative powers, that our Saviour sent the man to wash. It was a distance from the Temple area to Siloam, especially for a blind man, and all those whom he met along the way as a mud-smeared spectacle were witnesses of the miracle. But still the Jews would not believe, showing that they were blind in soul, whereas the man had been made whole both in soul and body.

Many other miracles have been worked here throughout the centuries. One can still see embedded in the wall a large column from a Justinian church built on the site. The Patriarchate of Jerusalem bought the property directly above the spring in order to rebuild the church. However, the Moslems prevented the building of the Orthodox Church by erecting a mosque nearby, for there is a law that no church can be built within a certain radius of a mosque.

Kontakion of the Sunday of the Blind Man
Fourth Tone
to "On this day Thou hast appeared"

Since my soul's noetic eyes are blind and sightless, I come unto Thee, O Christ, as did the man who was born blind. And in repentance I cry to Thee: Of those in darkness art Thou the most radiant Light.

Gethsemane

Gethsemane means "olive press" in Hebrew. From this we gather that there must have been olive groves and presses in the area. The Garden of Gethsemane, situated across the brook of Kedron from the Old City, was a favorite spot for our Saviour and the disciples. ("When Jesus had spoken these words, He went forth with His disciples over the brook Kedron, where was a garden, into the which He entered, and His disciples. And Judas also, which betrayed Him, knew the place: for Jesus ofttimes resorted thither with His disciples," St. John 18:1-2). The Kedron Valley was known in earlier times as the "Valley of Jehoshaphat." This is a combination of the Hebrew words *Jehovah* and *shaphot*, meaning "God judges," a name given to the place by the Prophet Joel (3:2). By tradition, the Last Judgment will take place in this area.

The entrance to the Crusader crypt church containing the Tomb of the Most Holy Mother of God.

THE TOMB OF THE MOTHER OF GOD

Tradition tells us that at the time of the Dormition of the Mother of God, she was carried in procession and laid in a tomb by the Apostles. The Apostle Thomas arrived late and requested that he might also bid her farewell. Upon opening her tomb, they found that her body was not there. A magnificent church was built over the tomb in the 5th century and destroyed in the 7th century by Chosroes the Persian; only the crypt of the church was preserved. To protect it, the Crusaders erected the existing building over the crypt. While descending the stairs into the crypt, one passes the tombs of

The front of the Tomb of the Most Holy Mother of God is covered with icons and tapestries. The original rock of the Tomb can be seen on the side walls.

Sts. Joachim and Anna on the right, and on the left, the tomb of St. Joseph the Betrothed. Being so far below street level, the crypt occasionally floods during the rainy season. The marble covering of the tomb was removed recently because of extensive water damage; it was then discovered that most of the original tomb was still intact. Christian chroniclers state that the tomb of the Mother of God had been taken to Constantinople, but to the joy of the faithful, only approximately a third of it had been removed. The remainder was encased in plexiglass.

✠

Dismissal Troparion of the Dormition of the Mother of God
First Tone
In giving birth thou didst preserve thy virginity; in thy dormition thou didst not forsake the world, O Theotokos. Thou wast translated unto life, since thou art the Mother of Life; and by thine intercessions dost thou redeem our souls from death.

✠

THE RUSSIAN CONVENT OF ST. MARY MAGDALENE

This traditional Russian church, replete with gold onion domes, was built by Tsar Alexander III to honor his mother and named for her patron Saint, St. Mary Magdalene. Grand Duchess Elizabeth was present at its consecration and expressed her fervent desire to be buried in the Holy Land. After she was martyred by the Bolsheviks in Alapaevsk in 1918, her relics and those of her faithful companion, the nun Barbara, were smuggled to the Holy Land. They now rest in reliquaries on either side of the iconostasis of this church. The Church celebrates their memory on July 5/18.

To the right of the main gates of the monastery are several shrines. The first one commemorates the words of our Saviour, "Watch and pray" (St. Matthew 26:41). The second contains the remains of an ancient set of stairs, traditionally thought to be where the donkey carrying our Saviour during His triumphal Entry into Jerusalem walked (St. Mark 11:7-11). Another large stone staircase weaves its way through lush gardens and monastery buildings to the church. A modest gift shop operates on the first level, while the church is located up another flight of stairs. Upon entering the church, one will notice over the Royal Gates a large icon of St. Mary Magdalene offering a red egg to Tiberius Caesar and proclaiming, "Christ is Risen!" According to tradition, she explained the teachings, miracles, betrayal and Resurrection of our Saviour to Tiberius, who then deprived Pilate of his authority and exiled him for his unjust administration. The convent also houses a miracle-working icon of the Mother of God that had become completely darkened; over a period of time, the icon renewed itself.

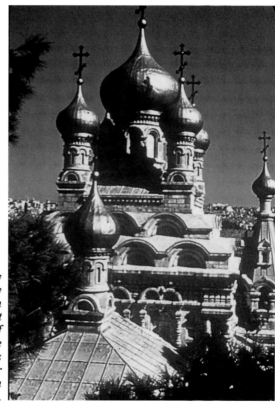

The Church of St. Mary Magdalene. Built by Tsar Alexander III in the late 19th century, it now houses the relics of the New Martyrs, the Grand Duchess Elizabeth and her companion, the nun Barbara.

40

The Mount of Olives

This mountain is actually a small mountain range with three summits; the southern summit was the site of the Ascension and subsequent home to all the Christian shrines on the mountain. A pilgrim of the 6th century writes of some twenty-four churches and shrines on the Mount of Olives. Most of these were completely destroyed during the Persian invasion in the 7th century. Our Lord must have traversed the Mount of Olives many times, and it is mentioned specifically in the New Testament several times: here our Lord discussed the end of the world with His disciples (St. Matthew 24), he withdrew here after preaching in the temple (St. Luke 21:37), and from here He ascended in glory (Acts 1:4-12).

ASCENSION

St. Luke 24:36-53

At that time, when Jesus had arisen from the dead, He stood in the midst of the disciples, and saith unto them, Peace be unto you. But they were terrified and affrighted, and supposed that they had seen a spirit. And He said unto them, Why are ye troubled? and why do thoughts arise in your hearts? Behold My hands and My feet, that it is I Myself: handle Me, and see; for a spirit hath not flesh and bones, as ye see Me have. And when He had thus spoken, He shewed them His hands and His feet. And while they yet believed not for joy, and wondered, He said unto them, Have ye here any meat? And they gave Him a piece of a broiled fish, and of an honeycomb. And He took it, and did eat before them. And He said unto them, These are the words which I spake unto you, while I was yet with you, that all things must be fulfilled, which were written in the law of Moses, and in the Prophets, and in the psalms, concerning Me. Then opened He their understanding, that they might understand the scriptures, and said unto them, Thus it is written, and thus it behoved Christ to suffer, and to rise from the dead the third day: And that repentance and remission of sins should be preached in His name among all nations, beginning at Jerusalem. And ye are witnesses of these things. And, behold, I send the promise of My Father upon you: but tarry ye in the city of Jerusalem, until ye be endued with power from on high. And He led them out as far as to Bethany, and He lifted up His hands, and blessed them. And it came to pass, while He blessed them, He was parted from them, and carried up into Heaven. And they worshipped Him, and returned to Jerusalem with great joy: And were continually in the temple, praising and blessing God. Amen.

Footprint of our Saviour left after His Ascension. The other footprint was taken to Constantinople as a blessing.

Ancient Church tradition states that when our Saviour ascended into the Heavens (St. Luke 24:36-53 and Acts 1:4-12), He left behind two footprints in the solid rock. One of them was subsequently cut out and taken to Constantinople, the other is enshrined inside the octagonal chapel. The original church on this site was built with a portion open to the sky. A system of mirrors magnified the light of oil lamps and reflected it through the opening in the roof so that from Jerusalem, Bethlehem, and Jericho one could see the light from this church. It was destroyed by the Persians in the 7th century, rebuilt, and destroyed many more times until Moslems seized the site and constructed a mosque there. Once each year, on Ascension, they permit the Orthodox Patriarch of Jerusalem to serve the Liturgy on the Holy Table behind the chapel. Some of the capitals are from Byzantine times and the walls of the enclosure contain the remains of ancient churches that were in the area.

This octagonal chapel on the Mount of Olives marks the place of our Lord's Ascension.

Dismissal Troparion of the Ascension
Fourth Tone

Thou hast ascended in glory, O Christ our God, and gladdened Thy disciples with the promise of the Holy Spirit; and they were assured by the blessing that Thou art the Son of God and Redeemer of the world.

✠

ST. PELAGIA'S TOMB

Just below the enclosure for the Ascension stands the mosque containing the tomb of St. Pelagia. Before St. Pelagia's conversion, she was a very beautiful and wealthy harlot who lived in the city of Antioch. When she heard the Christian teaching of the immortality of the soul and the Last Judgment, she repented with her whole soul. She gave away all her wealth and was baptized. On the eighth day after her baptism she disappeared. Several years later there was much talk in the Holy Land about a monk, Pelagius, who had enclosed himself in a small hut on the Mount of Olives. When Pelagius died, they found that he was actually a woman. This is the place of St. Pelagia's struggles in asceticism and her tomb. A mosque was built

The now empty tomb of St. Pelagia in the crypt of the mosque. Decorated cloths and bouquets of flowers have been left as offerings to the Saint.

over the shrine, enclosing it within a crypt. Once a year, on her Feast day (October 8/21), the Moslems open the gates for all Christians to venerate her tomb. At other times, arrangements to enter the tomb can be made with the guard at the Ascension shrine.

ELEON — THE RUSSIAN CONVENT OF THE ASCENSION

Visitors to this convent must phone ahead and receive permission for their visit, as the gate is kept locked. The main church, dedicated to the Ascension, was built on the remains of an ancient church which was the site of the martyrdom of many nuns by the Persians in 614. After slaughtering the nuns, the Persians set fire to

The main church at Eleon Convent dedicated to the Ascension, where the nuns were martyred in 614 by the Persians.

the church. The blood burned into the floor, leaving marks which are still evident in some areas of the church. In the church are several large icons, brought as gifts to the shrine by pious Russian pilgrims in the latter part of the last century. On the far side of the north wing of the church, framed by a railing, lies the grave of

Archimandrite Antonin, the first head of the Russian Ecclesiastical Mission. During some construction on the property, 5th and 6th century Byzantine remains were revealed. Among these are mosaic floors bearing Armenian inscriptions and ancient burial caves.

A small chapel marks the location where the head of St. John the Baptist was found. By tradition, Herod Antipas feared that if St. John's head was buried with his body, he would rise from the dead. His body was buried in Sebaste by his disciples, and his head was buried on the Mount of Olives. The location of the latter was lost

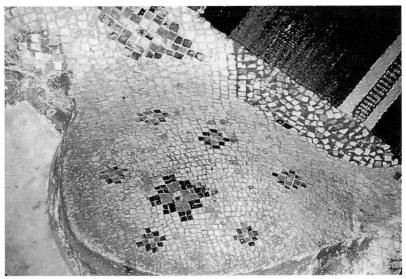

The head of St. John the Baptist was found in the place marked by the depression in the ancient mosaic floor.

until the 4th century, when a monastic named Innocent was digging and found the precious head of the Baptist. After the identity of the relic was revealed to him, he venerated it and reburied it in the same place. The Church celebrates the First and Second Finding of the Head of St. John the Baptist on February 24/March 9. The hollow seen in the 5th-7th century mosaic floor is the place where the head of the Forerunner was found.

On a clear day the convent's six-story bell tower can be seen even from Jordan. The panoramic view from the top of the tower is well worth the climb. The large bell from Russia was brought on foot from the Jaffa port in 1885 by pious pilgrims.

An extensive monastic cemetery contains the graves of the founders and former abbesses, including the grave of Abbess Tamara, daughter of Grand Duke Constantine Constantinovich Romanov. A woman of deep spiritual understanding, Abbess Tamara reposed on the Feast of the Dormition, August 15/28, 1979.

LITTLE GALILEE

Situated on the Mount of Olives, Little Galilee is so named because the residents of Galilee would camp there at the time of the Hebrew Passover, when the Law required their attendance in the Temple. At present, the property is owned by the Patriarchate of Jerusalem and is used as the summer residence of the Patriarch, as it is much cooler there than in the Old City. The first shrine on the left of the driveway commemorates the place where our Saviour

After His Resurrection, our Saviour appeared to the disciples who were gathered here.

partook of fish and honeycomb with His disciples after His Resurrection (St. Luke 24:42). Excavations in that area uncovered ruins of an ancient church with several columns. One of the columns has been enshrined.

Further down the path stands a chapel dedicated to and built on the site of the Second Annunciation of the Mother of God. Holy tradition tells us that the Mother of God lived on Mount Sion and would go daily to the site of her Son's Ascension, pray there, and return.

The church dedicated to the Second Annunciation of the Mother of God houses the grave of St. Susanna the Deaconess.

Before her Dormition the trees bent and reverenced her, and the Archangel Gabriel appeared and told her that she would repose in three days. She rejoiced and prepared for her departure, giving away her two tunics and visiting with the Apostles that were brought through the air in answer to her request.

Also inside this church is the grave of St. Susanna the Deaconess, who lived in the 3rd century. After her impious parents' death, she gave all her wealth to the poor, cut her hair, and entered a men's monastery. Through her great virtues, she became the superior of the monastery. After a scandal that caused her to reveal that she was a woman, she was ordained deaconess and wrought many miracles. Through her prayers, the idols fell. She was tortured for confessing Christ, but the tortures had no effect on her. She was cast into fire where, at peace, she surrendered her holy soul into the hands of God. St. Susanna is commemorated by the Orthodox Church on December 15/28.

Behind this chapel lies the grave of Abbot (†1959) Seraphim, abbot of the Seraphimo-Alexsev Monastery in the Perm district of Russia. He was one of the clergy who served the Romanov family in Ekaterinburg, their final place of imprisonment before they were martyred by the Bolsheviks in 1918. He was allowed to bring them Holy Communion, which was a great consolation for the family. A friend and confessor of the Grand Duchess Elizabeth, Abbot Seraphim was also able to serve her and the Romanov Grand Dukes who were held captive in Alapaevsk until their martyrdom, which was only twenty-four hours after the Tsar and his immediate family had been martyred. He accompanied the relics of Sts. Elizabeth and Barbara through many difficult circumstances to bring them to the Holy Land.

Since the Moslems have custody of the true site of the Ascension and only allow Liturgy to be served there once a year, the Patriarchate built the large church on the right side of the main driveway and dedicated it to the Ascension of our Lord.

Bethany

Scholars are now surmising that in the time of our Saviour, Bethany was actually a leper colony. The Law specified that a leper colony had to be a certain distance from a town and also downwind from the city, so that the breezes would not spread the disease. Ancient Bethany fulfills these specifications. In Arabic, the name of the city is Al-Azariyeh, a corruption of "Lazarus." Our Saviour came to Bethany many times to rest at the house of Lazarus with His disciples; here He was also a guest in the house of Simon the leper (St. Mark 14:3-9), and here He raised Lazarus from the dead (St. John 11:1-45).

THE TOMB OF LAZARUS

St. John 11:1-45

At that time, a certain man was sick, named Lazarus, of Bethany, the town of Mary and her sister Martha. (It was that Mary which anointed the Lord with ointment, and wiped His feet with her hair, whose brother Lazarus was sick.) Therefore his sisters sent unto Him, saying, Lord, behold, he whom Thou lovest is sick. When Jesus heard that, He said, This sickness is not unto death, but for the glory of God, that the Son of God might be glorified thereby. Now Jesus loved Martha, and her sister, and Lazarus. When He had heard therefore that he was sick, He abode two days still in the same place where He was. Then after that saith He to His disciples, Let us go into Judæa again. His disciples say unto Him, Master, the Jews of late sought to stone Thee; and goest Thou thither again? Jesus answered, Are there not twelve hours in the day? If any man walk in the day, he stumbleth not, because he seeth the light of this world. But if a man walk in the night, he stumbleth, because there is no light in him. These things said He: And after that He saith unto them, Our friend Lazarus sleepeth; but I go, that I may awake him out of sleep. Then said His disciples, Lord, if he sleep, he shall do well. Howbeit Jesus spake of his death: but they thought that He had spoken of taking of rest in sleep.

Then said Jesus unto them plainly, Lazarus is dead. And I am glad for your sakes that I was not there, to the intent ye may believe; nevertheless let us go unto him. Then said Thomas, which is called Didymus, unto his fellow disciples, Let us also go, that we may die with Him. Then when Jesus came, He found that he had lain in the grave four days already. Now Bethany was nigh unto Jerusalem, about fifteen furlongs off: And many of the Jews came to Martha and Mary, to comfort them concerning their brother. Then Martha, as soon as she heard that Jesus was coming, went and met Him: but Mary sat still in the house. Then said Martha unto Jesus, Lord, if Thou hadst been here, my brother had not died. But I know, that even now, whatsoever Thou wilt ask of God, God will give it Thee. Jesus saith unto her, Thy brother shall rise again. Martha saith unto Him, I know that he shall rise again in the resurrection at the last day. Jesus said unto her, I am the resurrection, and the life: he that believeth in Me, though he were dead, yet shall he live: And whosoever liveth and believeth in Me shall never die. Believest thou this? She saith unto Him, Yea, Lord: I believe that Thou art the Christ, the Son of God, Which should come into the world. And when she had so said, she went her way, and called Mary her sister secretly, saying, The Master is come, and calleth for thee. As soon as she heard that, she arose quickly, and came unto Him. Now Jesus was not yet come into the town, but was in that place where Martha met Him. The Jews then which were with her in the house, and comforted her, when they saw Mary, that she rose up hastily and went out, followed her, saying, She goeth unto the grave to weep there. Then when Mary was come where Jesus was, and saw Him, she fell down at His feet, saying unto Him, Lord, if Thou hadst been here, my brother had not died. When Jesus therefore saw her weeping, and the Jews also weeping which came with her, He groaned in the spirit, and was troubled, and said, Where have ye laid him? They said unto Him, Lord, come and see. Jesus wept. Then said the Jews, Behold how He loved him! And some of them said, Could not this man, which opened the eyes of the blind, have caused that even this man should not have died? Jesus therefore again groaning in Himself cometh to the grave. It was a cave, and a stone lay upon it. Jesus said, Take ye away the stone. Martha, the sister of him that was dead, saith unto Him, Lord, by this time he stinketh: for he hath been dead four days. Jesus saith unto her, Said I not unto thee, that, if thou wouldest believe, thou shouldest see the glory of God?

Then they took away the stone from the place where the dead was laid. And Jesus lifted up His eyes, and said, Father, I thank thee that Thou hast heard Me. And I knew that Thou hearest Me always: but because of the people which stand by I said it, that they may believe that Thou hast sent Me. And when He thus had spoken, He cried with a loud voice, Lazarus, come forth. And he that was dead came forth, bound hand and foot with graveclothes: and his face was bound about with a napkin. Jesus saith unto them, Loose him, and let him go. Then many of the Jews which came to Mary, and had seen the things which Jesus did, believed on Him.

"*In confirming the common resurrection, O Christ God, Thou didst raise up Lazarus from the dead before Thy Passion...*" (Dismissal Troparion of Lazarus Saturday). As a pledge and earnest of our resurrection at the end of time, Christ our God raised His friend Lazarus

The entrance to the crypt containing the tomb where Lazarus was buried for four days before our Lord restored him to life.

from the dead. The Church Fathers point out that even before physical death occurs, we each have our own Lazarus who is four days dead and stinketh — our soul, our heart, our mind. Yet there is hope, for as the sisters of Lazarus moved the Saviour to mercy by their tears, if we follow their example, He can be moved to resurrect us also.

Inside the tomb of Lazarus; the deeper section was the burial chamber.

Lazarus' tomb is owned by a Moslem family. They can be contacted at the souvenir shop directly across the way, and arrangements can be made to enter the tomb. The tomb is located underground, reached only by a very narrow and steep stairway hewn out of the rock. The tomb was enclosed and a large basilica was built to the east of it in the 4th century. This church was one of the few that was not destroyed in the Persian invasion in 614. However, after the Crusader defeat in the 12th century, the property fell into ruins. In the 16th century the Moslems built a mosque over the site, thwarting any attempt at rebuilding.

Dismissal Troparion of Lazarus Saturday
First Tone

In confirming the common Resurrection, O Christ God, Thou didst raise up Lazarus from the dead before Thy Passion. Wherefore we also, like the children, bearing the symbols of victory, cry to Thee, the Vanquisher of death: Hosanna in the highest; blessed is He that cometh in the Name of the Lord.

✠

BETHANY SCHOOL

The actual site where Martha and Mary met our Saviour on His way to resurrect Lazarus was lost for many centuries. The ruins of an ancient church, a cave church, and a stone with an ancient inscription in Greek were found in 1934 on the grounds of the Russian school in Bethany. The inscription says that this was the place where our Saviour met the sisters outside Bethany and proceeded to the Tomb of Lazarus. Here He told them, "I am the resurrection and the life" (St. John 11:25).

Across the street from the Russian School is the Greek Convent of St. Lazarus and his sisters, Sts. Martha and Mary. This was built before 1930 in accordance with the tradition that the meeting took place somewhere in the area.

Bethany School. The church is built on the site where our Saviour met Martha and Mary when He came to Bethany to raise Lazarus from the dead.

Katamon

THE MONASTERY OF ST. SYMEON THE GOD-RECEIVER

St. Luke 2:25-38

At that time, there was a man in Jerusalem, whose name was Simeon; and the same man was just and devout, waiting for the consolation of Israel: and the Holy Spirit was upon him. And it was revealed unto him by the Holy Spirit, that he should not see death, before he had seen the Lord's Christ. And he came by the Spirit into the temple: and when the parents brought in the child Jesus, to do for Him after the custom of the law, then took he Him up in his arms, and blessed God, and said, Lord, now lettest Thou Thy servant depart in peace, according to Thy word: For mine eyes have seen Thy salvation, which Thou hast prepared before the face of all people; a light to lighten the Gentiles, and the glory of Thy people Israel. And Joseph and His mother marvelled at those things which were spoken of Him. And Simeon blessed them, and said unto Mary His mother, Behold, this child is set for the fall and rising again of many in Israel; and for a sign which shall be spoken against; (Yea, a sword shall pierce through thy own soul also,) that the thoughts of many hearts may be revealed. And there was one Anna, a Prophetess, the daughter of Phanuel, of the tribe of Aser: she was of a great age, and had lived with an husband seven years from her virginity; and she was a widow of about fourscore and four years, which departed not from the temple, but served God with fastings and prayers night and day. And she coming in that instant gave thanks likewise unto the Lord, and spake of Him to all them that looked for redemption in Jerusalem.

The Monastery of St. Symeon the God-Receiver is tucked away in the residential neighborhoods of Katamon and the so-called Greek and German colonies. It was founded in the 11th century on the traditional site of the house of St. Symeon as a dependency of the Monastery of the Holy Cross.

Iconostasis of the church in the Monastery of St. Symeon the God-Receiver. St. Symeon's tomb is to the left of the iconostasis.

Inside the church, to the left of the iconostasis, is the empty tomb of St. Symeon. Several panel icons on the walls behind the tomb depict scenes from his life. St. Symeon was born in the 3rd century BC and was one of the seventy-two pious Hebrew scholars commissioned by the Egyptian king to translate the sacred books of the Jews into Greek, creating the Septuagint version of the Scriptures. When he was about to translate the passage, "Behold, a virgin shall conceive and bear a son" (Esaias 7:14), he was perplexed and wished to change the word "virgin" to "young woman." An Angel appeared to him, assured him of the accuracy of the prophecy, and added that St. Symeon would not die until he beheld the Messiah born of the Virgin. Still doubting, St. Symeon later took off his ring and cast it into a body of water, saying that if he saw his ring again it was possible that the prophecy would be fulfilled. He was amazed to see that when he cleaned and opened the fish bought for his supper, the ring was inside. St. Symeon waited patiently for the Messiah for many years, going daily to the Temple. At last the Child was brought to the Temple forty days after His birth according to the Law so that

He could be dedicated to God as the first-born male child of Mary, and also that she might offer the sacrifice of a pair of turtle doves or two young pigeons, as required by the Law. St. Symeon recognized the Messiah and took Him into his arms and said, "Lord, now lettest Thou Thy servant depart in peace..." (St. Luke 2:29).

Dismissal Troparion of the Meeting of the Lord in the Temple
First Tone

Rejoice, thou who art full of grace, O Virgin Theotokos, for from thee hath risen the Sun of Righteousness, Christ our God, enlightening those in darkness. Rejoice thou also, O righteous Elder, as thou receivest in thine arms the Redeemer of our souls, Who also granteth unto us the Resurrection.

The Monastery of the Holy Cross

In the sacred hymnology of the Church we hear about the Cross of our Lord being made of cypress, pine, and cedar wood, but only certain legends give an account of how this came to pass. This account describes Lot's task, as an epitemia for having sinned with his daughters, of watering the staffs of the three heavenly visitors to Abraham. The staffs were said to have sprouted as a sign of his forgiveness and grew together into one tree. This tree was said to have been cut down and brought for the rebuilding of the Temple. However, it remained unused until the soldiers used it much later to make the Cross. The Monastery of the Holy Cross is built over the site where this tree was planted. The place is located under the Holy Table in a chapel in a passageway behind the altar of the catholicon. Lining the walls of this passageway are glass cases containing many articles of interest, including embroidered vestments and old icons.

The Monastery of the Holy Cross. The bell tower and catholicon as seen from the courtyard.

The early history of the monastery is uncertain; however, 6th century mosaics were found during some restoration work. The catholicon and its mosaic floor date from 1040. The many frescoes surviving have Iberian inscriptions, as this monastery was a center of Georgian monasticism until the early 18th century. At that time, due to financial difficulties, the ownership of the monastery reverted to the Patriarchate of Jerusalem and a theological school was established. Today, it serves as a museum of the Patriarchate.

The iconostasis of the catholicon of the Monastery of the Holy Cross.

Dismissal Troparion of the Cross
First Tone

Save, O Lord, Thy people and bless Thine inheritance; grant Thou unto the faithful victory over adversaries. And by the power of Thy Cross, do Thou preserve Thy commonwealth.

✠

Judea

And thou, Bethlehem, house of Ephratha, art few in number to be reckoned among the thousands of Judah; yet out of thee shall One come forth to Me, to be a ruler of Israel; and His goings forth were from the beginning, even from Eternity. (Michaeas 5:2)

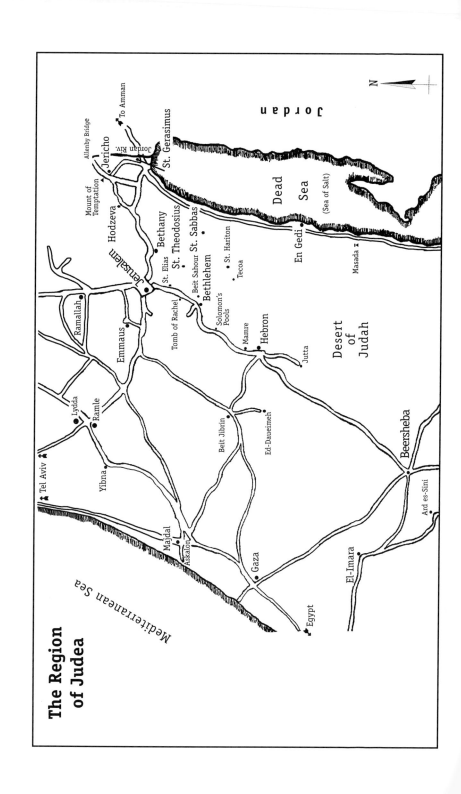

The Region of Judea

Mediterranean Sea

N

Jordan

Dead Sea (Sea of Salt)

Desert of Judah

To Amman
Allenby Bridge
St. Gerasimus
Jericho
Jordan Riv.
Mount of Temptation
Hodzeva
Bethany
St. Theodosius
St. Sabbas
Jerusalem
St. Elias
Beit Sahour
Bethlehem
St. Hariton
Tecoa
En Gedi
Masada
Tomb of Rachel
Solomon's Pools
Mamre
Hebron
Jutta
Ramallah
Emmaus
Lydda
Ramle
Beit Jibrin
Ed-Daueimeh
Beersheba
Ard es-Sini
Tel Aviv
Yibna
Majdal
Askalon
Gaza
Egypt
El-Imara

Bethlehem

"Bethlehem" means "house of bread," alluding to the large wheat fields that were in the area. It is also symbolic that our Saviour, the Bread of Life, came down from Heaven and made His abode there. Bethlehem was never enclosed by a wall; therefore it was taken by all invading armies. Present day Bethlehem is thought to be slightly to the East of the ancient city of David.

THE CHURCH OF THE NATIVITY

St. Matthew 2:1-12

Now when Jesus was born in Bethlehem of Judæa in the days of Herod the king, behold, there came wise men from the east to Jerusalem, saying, Where is He that is born King of the Jews? for we have seen His star in the east, and are come to worship Him. When Herod the king had heard these things, he was troubled, and all Jerusalem with him. And when he had gathered all the chief priests and scribes of the people together, he demanded of them where Christ should be born. And they said unto him, In Bethlehem of Judæa: for thus it is written by the Prophet, And thou Bethlehem, in the land of Juda, art not the least among the princes of Juda: for out of thee shall come a Governor, that shall rule My people Israel. Then Herod, when he had privily called the wise men, enquired of them diligently what time the star appeared. And he sent them to Bethlehem, and said, Go and search diligently for the young child; and when ye have found Him, bring me word again, that I may come and worship Him also. When they had heard the king, they departed; and, lo, the star, which they saw in the east, went before them, till it came and stood over where the young child was. When they saw the star, they rejoiced with exceeding great joy. And when they were come into the house, they saw the young child with Mary His mother, and fell down, and worshipped Him: and when they had opened their treasures, they presented unto Him gifts; gold, and frankincense, and myrrh. And being warned of God in a dream that they should not return to Herod, they departed into their own country another way.

In Bethlehem at the time of our Saviour it was common for poor people to live in caves. Even today, caves are homes for many. They often keep their animals in a lower cave, while an upper cave is used for living quarters. St. Luke records in his Gospel, "And she brought forth her first-born Son, and wrapped Him in swaddling clothes and laid Him in a manger; because there was no room for them in the inn" (2:7). St. Joseph obtained permission for them to stay in the cave with the animals and it was here that our Saviour chose to be born of the Ever-Virgin.

The Church of the Nativity of our Saviour in Bethlehem.

In the year 135 the Emperor Hadrian planted a grove dedicated to the pagan god Adonis and established pagan rites in the cave of the Nativity of our Saviour. St. Helen ordered the destruction of the "sacred" grove and the cleansing of the cave in 324. She then had a large, richly adorned basilica built on the site, with an octagonal structure above the actual cave. Through an opening in the center of the octagon, one could see into the cave below. In the mid-6th century, the Emperor Justinian remodelled the church, enlarging it and building a fortified monastery for the monks living there. The

Interior of the Church of the Nativity of our Saviour. The entrance to the Cave of the Nativity is located to the right of the iconostasis.

architectural structures seen today are largely from Justinian's time, but many of the original decorations of the church have been pillaged over the centuries. To preserve the elaborate mosaic floor from St. Helen's church, a wooden plank floor was constructed with several trap-doors which can be opened to reveal the beautiful floor underneath. Since it was a common practice of invading armies to house their animals in the churches, the main entrance was partially blocked to prevent this, requiring one to bend over to enter. To the right of the main aisle, a large stone baptistery can be seen with the inscription, *"In memory of and for the repose and remission of the sins of those whose names the Lord knows."* Only a small portion of the wall mosaics commissioned in 1169 have survived. Above the pillars in the nave, the Seven Ecumenical Councils and Seven Regional Councils were depicted with their key decisions inscribed in Greek. The rest of the interior walls were covered with scenes from the life and miracles of our Saviour as well as figures of Prophets, Saints, and Angels.

The **Cave of the Nativity of our Saviour** is reached by descending the narrow staircase to the right of the iconostasis and platform. The place where our Lord was born is on the right side, marked by a marble slab with a silver star and ringed by numerous oil lamps. The silver star with the words engraved in Latin, "Here Jesus Christ was born to the Virgin Mary," was added by the Latins in 1717. To the left, they have designated the "Place of the Manger" and have built an altar there.

In the Cave of the Nativity, numerous oil lamps ring the place where Christ was born.

✠

Dismissal Troparion of the Nativity
Fourth Tone

Thy nativity, O Christ our God, hath shined the light of knowledge upon the world; for thereby they that worshipped the stars were instructed by a star to worship Thee, the Sun of Righteousness, and to know Thee, the Dayspring from on high. O Lord, glory be to Thee.

✠

THE CAVE OF THE HOLY INNOCENTS

St. Matthew 2:13-23

When the wise men were departed, behold, the Angel of the Lord appeareth to Joseph in a dream, saying, Arise, and take the young child and His mother, and flee into Egypt, and be thou there until I bring thee word: for Herod will seek the young child to destroy Him. When he arose, he took the young child and His mother by night, and departed into Egypt: And was there until the death of Herod: that it might be fulfilled which was spoken of the Lord by the Prophet, saying, Out of Egypt have I called My son. Then Herod, when he saw that he was mocked of the wise men, was exceeding wroth, and sent forth, and slew all the children that were in Bethlehem, and in all the coasts thereof, from two years old and under, according to the time which he had diligently enquired of the wise men. Then was fulfilled that which was spoken by Jeremiah the Prophet, saying, In Rama was there a voice heard, lamentation, and weeping, and great mourning, Rachel weeping for her children, and would not be comforted, because they are not. But when Herod was dead, behold, an Angel of the Lord appeareth in a dream to Joseph in Egypt, saying, Arise, and take the young child and His mother, and go into the land of Israel: for they are dead which sought the young child's life. And he arose, and took the young Child and His mother, and came into the land of Israel. But when he heard that Archelaus did reign in Judæa in the room of his father Herod, he was afraid to go thither: notwithstanding, being warned of God in a dream, he turned aside into the parts of Galilee: And he came and dwelt in a city called Nazareth: that it might be fulfilled which was spoken by the Prophets, He shall be called a Nazarene.

An oral tradition was passed down through many generations that the place being used as a garbage dump outside the Church of the Nativity was actually a holy site. In the early 1960's the site was excavated revealing catacombs, a crypt, graves, a Holy Table, and many bones. Investigation showed that most of the bones were from children under the age of two, although there were also many bones from older children. It was surmised that these were many of the Holy Innocents, the children killed by Herod's armies. Presumably, other children were buried with the Innocents by their relatives so they would be close to the relics. Early Christians gathered in the catacombs and served Liturgy near the relics. The Holy Innocents are commemorated on December 29/January 11.

Dismissal Troparion of the Holy Innocents
First Tone

As acceptable victims, as newly-picked flowers and divine first fruits and newborn lambs were ye offered unto Christ Who was born as an infant, O pure Infants. And ye rebuked Herod's wickedness and unceasingly pray in behalf of our souls.

Beit Sahour

SHEPHERDS' FIELD

St. Luke 2:1-20

And it came to pass in those days, that there went out a decree from Cæsar Augustus, that all the world should be taxed. (And this taxing was first made when Cyrenius was governor of Syria.) And all went to be taxed, every one into his own city. And Joseph also went up from Galilee, out of the city of Nazareth, into Judæa, unto the city of David, which is called Bethlehem; (because he was of the house and lineage of David:) To be taxed with Mary his espoused wife, being great with child. And so it was, that, while they were there, the days were accomplished that she should be delivered. And she brought forth her firstborn son, and wrapped Him in swaddling clothes, and laid Him in a manger; because there was no room for them in the inn. And there were in the same country shepherds abiding in the field, keeping watch over their flock by night. And, lo, the Angel of the Lord came upon them, and the glory of the Lord shone round about them: and they were sore afraid. And the Angel said unto them, Fear not: for, behold, I bring you good tidings of great joy, which shall be to all people. For unto you is born this day in the city of David a Saviour, which is Christ the Lord. And this shall be a sign unto you; Ye shall find the babe wrapped in swaddling clothes, lying in a manger. And suddenly there was with the Angel a multitude of the heavenly host praising God, and saying, Glory to God in the highest, and on earth peace, good will toward men. And it came to pass, as the Angels were gone away from them into Heaven, the shepherds said one to another, Let us now go even unto Bethlehem, and see this thing which is come to pass, which the Lord hath made known unto us. And they came with haste, and found Mary, and Joseph, and the Babe lying in a manger. And when they had seen it, they made known abroad the saying which was told them concerning this Child. And all they that heard it wondered at those things which were told them by the shepherds. But Mary kept all these things, and pondered them in her heart. And the

shepherds returned, glorifying and praising God for all the things that
they had heard and seen, as it was told unto them.

After worshipping the Lord in Beth-el, the Patriarch Jacob travelled with his family toward Bethlehem. On the way, his beloved wife, Rachel, gave birth to Benjamin and then died. Jacob buried her and set a pillar upon her grave and continued his journey. He camped near the **Tower of Edar** and bought land on which he grew wheat and barley (Genesis 35). The tower served as a vantage point from which to watch over his fields. In later years, it was customary to climb the tower to look toward Bethlehem, whence the Messiah was to come. (The base of this tower can still be seen to the left of the stairs leading to the crypt church.) Ruth the Moabite gleaned in these fields, which had passed as an inheritance to Boaz, and she attracted his attention by her modesty and sobriety. He married her and she bore Obed, the grandfather of Prophet David. David played his harp while tending his father's sheep in these fields.

At the time of Christ, these fields were used for grazing. Some sources state that the sheep bought for sacrifice in the Temple were always taken from the sheep grazing here. The shepherds from this area were descendants of David; they were peaceful and pure of heart, unlike the shepherds from the neighboring villages. Thus they were worthy to hear the Angels and to worship and receive the King of Peace. On the night our Saviour was born, the shepherds were keeping watch over their sheep. A bright light appeared, and they saw the Angels and were frightened. The Archangel Gabriel told them of the birth of the Messiah, saying, "Fear not..." (St. Luke 2:10). They left their flocks and walked to Bethlehem to find the Saviour. The cave, the manger, the swaddling clothes, all served to prove the identity of the young Child. Many of the mother-of-pearl carvers now living here are descendants of the shepherds and they always include at least one shepherd in their carvings of the Nativity scene.

Local residents have called these fields "of the All-holy One" because, during the flight into Egypt, the Family passed through them. The Mother of God has appeared throughout the centuries walking through these properties, sometimes as Queen, and sometimes as a nun.

This property is a metochion of St. Sabbas' monastery. The Orthodox have always known that this is the authentic Shepherds' Field. In fact, St. Helen built the crypt church which has been used as a parish church by the Arab Christians for centuries. In 1972 excavations at the site revealed that there were ruins of churches from the 4th, 5th, and 6th centuries, as well as ruins of a monastery from the 7th century, proving that this was indeed the original site. Mosaics were uncovered with Greek inscriptions, *"Remember, O Lord, Thy servant Lazarus, and for his fruition,"* and also, *"Remember, O Lord, Hesychius. . ."* These were the founders of the church in the monastery that was destroyed when the Persians attacked and killed the one hundred monks living there. The bone room with the relics of these fathers was found on the far side of the church.

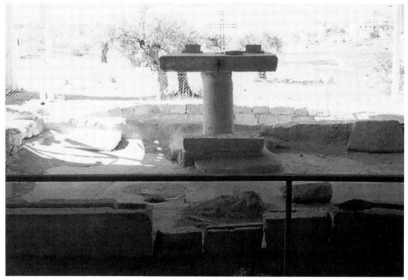

Excavations of a 6th-century Byzantine church at Shepherds' Field.

The crypt church can be dated to the 4th century, the time of St. Helen, by the inlaid crosses in the mosaic floor; later canons prohibited using the Cross to decorate the floor. The floor has been covered to protect the mosaic, but as in the Church of the Nativity, several trap doors open to reveal the beautiful floor beneath. According to tradition, the shepherds wanted to be buried where they heard the

Angels' glad tidings. Their grave is at the back of the church between the two pillars. To protect the extensive ruins, when the need arose for a larger church for the community, the new church was not built above the crypt church, but a short distance away.

The modern iconostasis of the 4th-century crypt church in Shepherds' Field.

Hebron

Hebron, one of the oldest cities in the Holy Land and the highest above sea level (3000 ft/914 m), lies along the road from Bethlehem to Beersheeba. When God told the Patriarch Abraham, "Arise, walk through the land in the length of it and the breadth of it; for I will give it unto thee" (Genesis 13:17), he pitched his tent in the Plain of Mamre, a little north of Hebron, and built an altar to the Lord. There he gave hospitality under a large oak tree to the three heavenly visitors, who foretold the birth of Isaac (Genesis 18:1-15). When Sarah died, Abraham bought a field with a cave, the **Cave of Machpelah**, to be a burial place for his family (Genesis 23:19). Abraham and Isaac and his wife, Rebecca, lived in the environs of Mamre and were buried in the Cave of Machpelah. When Jacob returned from dwelling near Bethlehem, he lived near Mamre until his son Joseph brought the family into Egypt (Genesis 46:5-27). After Jacob reposed in Egypt, his sons buried him in the Cave of Machpelah with his forefathers and his first wife, Leah (Genesis 50:7-13).

When the children of Israel returned to the Promised Land after their four-hundred-year sojourn in Egypt, Joshua gave the city of Hebron as an inheritance to Caleb (Joshua 15:13). Later, it was given to the sons of Aaron. Hebron was also a "city of refuge;" anyone who accidentally killed someone could take refuge there and legally be protected from revenge. In Hebron, the Prophet King David was anointed King of Israel (II Kings 2). He also had his capital there for seven and a half years before it was moved to Jerusalem.

Hebron, also known by the Arabic name Al-Khalil ("The Friend," in homage to Abraham, "The Friend of the Lord"), is almost entirely Moslem, and, as of this writing, the political atmosphere in the area is extremely tense. Pilgrims are advised to contact a local tour agency if they wish to visit Hebron.

THE TOMB OF THE PATRIARCHS

The Cave of Machpelah is the burial place of three pairs of Patriarchs and Matriarchs: Abraham and Sarah, Isaac and Rebecca, and Isaac's son Jacob, and Leah, as well as some of the sons of Jacob. Situated in the center of Hebron, the shrine is sacred to Christians, Moslems and Jews. The present large building over the cave was originally built by Herod the Great. Over the centuries, the structure was adapted many times. As political power in the Holy Land shifted from one religion to another, it was converted into a place of worship for the members of the ruling religion. At present, a mosque and a synagogue occupy the site. Cenotaphs mark the site of the underground burial chamber which has been sealed for many centuries. The first pair of cenotaphs that the pilgrim will encounter is that of Abraham and Sarah. To the right is that of Jacob and Leah, and to the left, within the main mosque, is that of Isaac and Rebecca. Under the red and white stone structures, the Patriarchs' cenotaphs have green coverings, while their wives' coverings are purple. Pilgrims should be aware that the guardians of the shrine are zealous Moslems who strictly forbid anyone to make the sign of the Cross in the enclosure.

THE PLAIN OF MAMRE

About two miles north of Hebron, on a high hill east of the main Jerusalem–Hebron road, is the site identified as the Plain of Mamre, where Abraham had camped. Mamre was held sacred by the Jews as early as the 9th century BC. The Emperor Hadrian built an enclosure wall and a temple to Hermes at the site in about 130 AD. St. Constantine destroyed the pagan temple and built a large church on the eastern side of the enclosure in the 4th century. The western part contained the Oak of Mamre, Abraham's altar, and the well which Abraham had dug. This church was an important religious center from the 4th century until at least the 8th century. Archaeologists have extensively excavated this site and uncovered the remains of the enclosure wall, the church, including inscriptions and capitals of columns, and the well in the southwest corner of the enclosure.

THE MONASTERY OF THE HOLY FOREFATHERS

West of the town of Hebron, closer to the road, is the Russian Orthodox Monastery of the Holy Forefathers. Built in 1871, it served as a hostel for Russian pilgrims for many years. For nearly 35 years, until his repose in 1986, the abbot was Archimandrite Ignaty. Known for his bounteous hospitality to all pilgrims, his great love for and faith in the Mother of God, as well as his holy life, Fr. Ignaty was also loved and respected by the local Moslem population.

A possible descendent of the Oak of Mamre. Under the Oak of Mamre, Abraham gave hospitality to the three heavenly visitors (Genesis 18).

On the property is an ancient oak tree, thought to be a descendent of the Oak of Mamre. Although it appears to be dead, the huge tree, supported by scaffolding, sends forth new shoots from time to time. Among the Russian people there exists the pious belief that the death of this tree will signify the end of the world. It is not known, however, how this belief arose.

The Monastery of St. Sabbas

Built on the steep slope of the Kedron Valley, in what used to be the heart of the wilderness between Bethlehem and the Dead Sea, the Lavra of St. Sabbas (also called the Great Lavra) is the most important monastery in the Judean desert. It has enjoyed an uninterrupted history of some 1,510 years. Founded by St. Sabbas in 485, after others came to share his life in the wilderness, the monastery has also been the home of many other important Saints of the Church, including: St. John of Damascus the hymnographer and historian, St. John of Kolonia, St. Cosmas the Hymnographer, St. Stephen the Wonderworker, St. Michael Syngelus, St. Theophanes, St. Cyril of Scythopoulos, and St. Theodore of Edessa.

The Great Lavra of St. Sabbas the Sanctified consists of many structures built into the steep western slope of the Kedron Valley.

The cave where St. Sabbas spent five years struggling alone can still be seen opposite the monastery towards the east, with an iron grating in the window that has a Cross and the Greek letters *"Я"* and "**C**" (the initials for "Saint Sabbas" in Greek) worked into it. In need of water, St. Sabbas prayed to God from his cave and saw in the moonlight a wild ass digging in the soil with its hooves. When it had made quite a deep hole, he saw it drink from the hole. St. Sabbas understood that God had sent them water; he dug at the place and found a spring of water that still exists, being neither too abundant in winter nor scarce in summer. This spring is located in a small chapel at the base of the monastery, at the bottom of the ravine.

The incorrupt relics of St. Sabbas the Sanctified in the church now dedicated to him. The relics, which had been taken by the Crusaders to the West, were returned to the Lavra in 1965.

Another night St. Sabbas left his cave and, while in prayer, saw a pillar of fire on the western slope of the ravine, where his tomb now stands between the two churches. After having continued in prayer in this place until dawn, he found a large and wondrous cave which had the shape of a church. Thanking God, St. Sabbas held the church services there. This church is known as *Theoktistos* (God-built) and is dedicated to St. Nicholas. Some of the murals date to Byzantine times. Along the walls glass cases contain the skulls of the fathers that were martyred in this area. The ancient burial place of the monastery is located under the courtyard where the chapel over the grave of St. Sabbas is found. Depictions of St. Sabbas in the tomb and frescoes of the Saints who were sanctified in the monastery cover the walls of the chapel.

In the ravine to the far right of the cave of St. Sabbas is an enclosure marking the cave of St. John of Kolonia, also called "the Hesychast." St. John fled his episcopal throne and, hiding his rank, asked for admission into St. Sabbas' monastery. After many years, St. Sabbas took St. John to Jerusalem to have him ordained. St. John told the Patriarch privately that he was already a bishop and therefore could not be ordained a priest. The Patriarch told St. Sabbas that he could not ordain the man and sent them home. Crushed by this unexpected impediment, St. Sabbas prayed and the matter was revealed to him, whereupon he loved and honored St. John greatly. After the death of St. Sabbas, St. John strengthened the faith of the brothers when the region was raided by barbarians. The Church celebrates his memory on December 3/16.

As the lavra grew and the church became too cramped for their numbers, St. Sabbas built another church beside the cave church. This catholicon was originally dedicated to the Annunciation, but after the repose of St. Sabbas, the Mother of God appeared to the new abbot and requested that it be rededicated in honor of St. Sabbas. In this we see the special love of the Mother of God for St. Sabbas. Every monastery in the Holy Land dedicated its catholicon to the Theotokos in order to combat the heresies of the Origenists, Arians, and Nestorians, which deny the divinity of our Saviour. Without her express approval, the monastery would not have rededicated the church to St. Sabbas. This church now houses the incorrupt relics of St. Sabbas which are a source of miracles for all that turn to him in faith. To the left of the small narthex is another narthex with a fresco of the Akathist Hymn, before which the fathers of the monastery say the Akathist every evening. Compline is held here also.

A chapel incorporating the tomb of St. John of Damascus and his cave cell is found on a different, higher level in the monastery. St. John was an eminent official of the Moslem court in Damascus and a wise apologist for the Orthodox. After an intrigue at court, which caused him to lose his right hand, he entreated the Mother of God

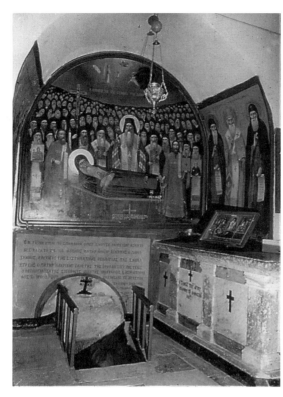

The chapel incorporating the tomb and cave of St. John of Damascus. Among the works of St. John still in use in the Church are canons for many of the feasts, including the joyous Paschal Canon, which begins, "It is the day of Resurrection, let us be radiant, O ye people. . ."

and she restored it to its place. St. John then appealed to the caliph to dismiss him from his service so that he might serve God. After giving away all his wealth, he and his adopted brother, St. Cosmas, retired to the Monastery of St. Sabbas. Here St. John was entrusted to the care of a simple elder who did not allow him to write or chant anything, for the sake of obedience and humility. After an incident in which St. John composed a hymn for one of the brothers without a blessing, the elder cast him out of their cell. As an epitemia, St. John cleaned the latrines of the lavra with his hands. Moved by his humility, the elder received him back and, after a vision of the Mother of God, begged St. John to continue to write hymns and treatises for the edification of the faithful. St. John, with the help of his foster brother, St. Cosmas, composed a vast number of hymns, canons, and patristic works, many of which are still in use in the Orthodox Church today. The memory of St. John of Damascus is celebrated by the Church on December 4/17.

The mother of St. Sabbas, St. Sophia, requested that she be allowed to live close to her son. Since he never allowed any woman to enter the monastery, St. Sabbas had a tower built for her, which can be seen to the right of the monastery as one faces the Kedron Valley. Following his example, women are not allowed to enter the monastery, but they are allowed to visit the spring at the base of the monastery by following the path to the right of the courtyard.

Throughout the centuries, the monks living here have been subjected to countless attacks, plunders, and slaughters. Some of the skulls of the martyred fathers can be seen in a deep recess in the cavern church. In order to be given warning of an attack, the monks have placed loose stones on top of the outer walls of the monastery. In the event that someone places a ladder against them, the stones come crashing down, making enough noise to sound the alarm.

Approximately one hundred fifty monks lived in the Lavra at the time of St. Sabbas, and the monastery started to increase after the Persian invasion (614) and the Arab conquest (638). The largest population was seen during the 8th and 9th centuries. In the 19th century the monastery was rebuilt with funds from Imperial Russia and reconstructed as a fortress on four levels.

Dismissal Troparion of St. Sabbas the Sanctified
Plagal of Fourth Tone (8th)

With the stream of thy tears, thou didst cultivate the barrenness of the desert; and by thy sighings from the depths, thou didst bear fruit a hundredfold in labours; and thou becamest a luminary, shining with miracles upon the world, O Sabbas our righteous Father. Intercede with Christ God that our souls be saved.

✠

The Monastery of St. Theodosius the Cenobiarch

St. Theodosius the Cenobiarch, or leader of the cenobitic monastics, was born in Cappadocia. As a youth he conceived a longing to visit the Holy Land and become a monastic. He went to Antioch to seek the blessing of St. Symeon the Stylite. St. Symeon greeted him by name and foretold all that he would accomplish; that is, he would be a great light for the faithful and a leader of monastics. Encouraged by the prayers and blessings of St. Symeon, St. Theodosius went to the Holy Land and placed himself in obedience to an experienced ascetic, the elder Longinus. After living with him for some years and acquiring many of the virtues, St. Theodosius fled the praise of men and retired to a small cave. Many wishing to become monks gathered around him and entreated him to build a monastery. St. Theodosius took a censer, and placing in it unlit charcoal and incense, prayed to God that He show him the site

The Monastery of St. Theodosius. The church is in the background.

81

designated for the monastery by igniting the charcoal and sending forth smoke from the incense. As he and several disciples traversed the desert near Bethlehem, the coal lit itself near a cave, sending forth the fragrance of incense. The brethren immediately set about laying the foundation and building the necessary structures for the monastery. God revealed to St. Theodosius that the cave was the place where the Magi stopped for the night on their way back to their own country after worshipping our Saviour in Bethlehem (St. Matthew 2:12).

The cave where the Magi spent the night when they returned to Persia. The niches in the wall contain tombs.

Founded in 465, this monastery was the center for cenobitic monasticism, just as St. Sabbas' was for anchorites. At its height, this monastery housed approximately seven hundred monks of various nationalities and carried on many philanthropic duties. The Persian invaders and later the Arab conquerors martyred many fathers and scattered a great number of the rest, so that until the 16th century only a handful remained. For the next four hundred years, the monastery remained uninhabited, and the buildings were used by members of the Ibn-Abbed tribe as shelters for their sheep (hence the

Arabic name of the monastery, Ibn-Abbed Monastery). In 1858, the ruined monastery was purchased by the Patriarchate and a series of restorations and rebuilding was begun. Presently, the monastery is occupied by a small group of nuns.

In the monastery the catholicon is dedicated to the Annunciation of the Mother of God. Below the traditional depiction of the Annunciation on the Royal Doors is a representation of the Magi entering a cave.

The **Cave of the Magi** is reached from the courtyard by descending a short flight of stairs. In a niche in the wall on the left as one is descending are relics of the fathers that were martyred by the invaders. A small Holy Table with an iconostasis make it possible to serve the Liturgy near the relics. Alcoves in the wall contain the tombs of the following righteous ones: St. Theodosius; St. Sophronius, a former abbot of the monastery and later Patriarch of Jerusalem; St. Eulogia, the mother of St. Theodosius; St. Sophia, the mother of St. Sabbas; St. Theodote, the mother of Sts. Cosmas and Damian; St. Maria, the wife of St. Xenophon and the mother of Sts. Arcadius and John; and John Moscos, the author of *Spiritual Meadows*.

Dismissal Troparion of St. Theodosius the Cenobiarch
Plagal of First Tone (5th)

Having shown forth in God-given virtues, O righteous one, thou didst prove to be an illustrious model of the monastic life. And thou wast seen to be a God-like luminary and leader, O wise Father Theodosius, emulator of the angels, and servant of the Trinity. Do thou beseech our God unceasingly that He have mercy on our souls.

✠

Emmaus

St. Luke 24:12-35

At that time, Peter arose and ran unto the sepulchre; and stooping down, he beheld the linen clothes laid by themselves, and departed, wondering in himself at that which was come to pass. And, behold, two of them went that same day to a village called Emmaus, which was from Jerusalem about threescore furlongs. And they talked together of all these things which had happened. And it came to pass, that, while they communed together and reasoned, Jesus Himself drew near, and went with them. But their eyes were holden that they should not know Him. And He said unto them, What manner of communications are these that ye have one to another, as ye walk, and are sad? And the one of them, whose name was Cleopas, answering said unto Him, Art Thou only a stranger in Jerusalem, and hast not known the things which are come to pass there in these days? And He said unto them, What things? And they said unto Him, Concerning Jesus of Nazareth, which was a Prophet mighty in deed and word before God and all the people: and how the chief priests and our rulers delivered Him to be condemned to death, and have crucified Him. But we trusted that it had been He which should have redeemed Israel: and beside all this, to day is the third day since these things were done. Yea, and certain women also of our company made us astonished, which were early at the sepulchre; and when they found not His body, they came, saying, that they had also seen a vision of Angels, which said that He was alive. And certain of them which were with us went to the sepulchre, and found it even so as the women had said: but Him they saw not. Then He said unto them, O fools, and slow of heart to believe all that the Prophets have spoken: ought not Christ to have suffered these things, and to enter into His glory? And beginning at Moses and all the Prophets, He expounded unto them in all the scriptures the things concerning Himself. And they drew nigh unto the village, whither they went: and He made as though He would have gone further. But they constrained Him, saying, Abide with us: for it is toward evening, and the day is far spent. And He went in to tarry with them. And it came to pass, as He sat at meat with them, He took bread, and blessed it, and brake, and gave to them. And their eyes were opened, and they knew Him; and He vanished out of their sight. And they said one to another, Did not our heart burn within us, while He talked with us by the way, and while He opened to us the scriptures? And they rose up the same hour, and returned to Jerusalem, and found the eleven gathered together, and them that were with them, saying, The Lord is risen indeed, and hath appeared to Simon. And they told what things were done in the way, and how He was made known unto them in the breaking of the bread.

The ruins of the Crusader church at Emmaus.

Approximately seven miles or "threescore furlongs" from Jerusalem lies the village of Emmaus. The villa where our Lord broke bread with the Apostles Luke and Cleopas after their journey was later used as a meeting place by the early Christians. A Byzantine basilica with a large complex of buildings was built on top of, or incorporating, the ruins of this villa. Excavations have uncovered the remains of numerous later churches. The massive walls seen today were part of a smaller Romanesque-style church built by the Crusaders over the remains of the Byzantine basilica, incorporating the original apse. Many large portions of intact mosaic floors, as well the baptistry with a cruciform baptismal font, have been uncovered.

An ancient cruciform baptistry is found among the excavated ruins of the church at Emmaus.

A Syriac homily likens the life of a Christian to the walk to Emmaus, saying that without true, burning love for God, our neighbor, and all creation, we will never attain that burning heart without which we cannot be true Christians. St. John of Kronstadt wrote in *My Life in Christ,* "When you feel in your heart that the Lord 'makes as though He would go further' from your heart, from your thoughts, then constrain Him, the Merciful One, saying sincerely: 'Abide with me: for it is toward evening and the day' of my spiritual life 'is far spent; and He shall come in to tarry with thee;' for He is merciful, and lets Himself be constrained."[1]

---

[1] St. John of Kronstadt, My Life in Christ, (Jordanville, NY: Holy Trinity Monastery, 1984), p. 536.

Fifth Exapostilarion

Lo, Christ Who is the Life and Way, from the dead having risen, with Cleopas and Luke did walk; and He was made known unto them at Emmaus when He brake the bread; though within them were kindled most fervently their hearts and souls when to them He was speaking along the way, and from Holy Writ explained what He had suffered. With them let us cry: He arose and appeared unto Peter.

✠

Lуσσα
(Loσ)

THE TOMB OF ST. GEORGE

Near the Ben-Gurion Airport lies the ancient city of Lod, or Lydda. St. Peter came to Lydda two years after our Saviour's Resurrection and healed the paralytic Aeneas (Acts 9:33-34). St. George the Great Martyr was born in Lydda and, while serving in the Roman army, was brought to trial for his faith in Christ and

Iconostasis of the Church of St. George in Lydda.

martyred. Before his death in the early 4th century, he requested that his servant bring his body back to his homeland. The Christian community in Lydda grew and in 325 its bishop attended the First Ecumenical Council. St. Helen built a large basilica over the tomb of St. George that attracted many pilgrims from different countries.

The Crusaders rebuilt the church which had been destroyed in the Arab conquest and constructed a fortified cathedral. The knights then chose St. George as their patron Saint, and during the third Crusade, King Richard the Lion-Hearted adopted him as the patron Saint of England. The cathedral was destroyed by the invading

The reliquary of the Holy Great Martyr George is a site of many healings.

Mamelukes in 1260. Because St. George worked so many miracles for the Moslems, in 1268 they built a large mosque on part of the ruins of the cathedral which incorporated stonework from the earlier churches. In 1870 the Orthodox received permission to build a church on the remaining portion of the ruins next to the mosque. The tomb of St. George is in a crypt in this church. The British Mandate Government had a great reverence for St. George and celebrated his feast by sending representatives with gifts to the church.

In addition to the many miracles that St. George works daily for all who call on him with faith, in this church St. George often heals those suffering from demonic possession. For this purpose, a set of chains in which the demonized are restrained has been attached to a column on the wall to the right of the iconostasis.

Dismissal Troparion of St. George the Great Martyr
Fourth Tone

Liberator of captives, defender of the poor, physician of the sick, and champion of kings, O trophy-bearer Great Martyr George, intercede with Christ God that our souls be saved.

Hoᴅzeʋa

THE MONASTERY OF ST. GEORGE OF HODZEVA

The Monastery of St. George of Hodzeva is situated on the northern side of the steep cliff of the Wadi Kelt, the deep gorge which connects Jerusalem with Jericho. Carved in arid, desert landscapes by ancient water courses, wadis typically transform into fast flowing rivers after torrential rain storms. According to living tradition, near the monastery is the ancient "Aenon" mentioned in the Gospel of St. John (3:23), where St. John the Baptist was baptizing because there was "much water." The Judean desert, through which the wadi winds, has been home to many Old Testament solitaries such as Elias, Elisseus, and the sons of the Prophets. Our Saviour prayed and rested here many times, as did St. John the Baptist. Until the Persian invasion, this desert was densely populated by monastics.

The Monastery of St. George Hodzeva on the road from Jerusalem to Jericho as seen from the opposite side of the ravine. The surrounding cliffs are honeycombed with caves once inhabited by monks.

The Romans were renowned for their skillful building of roads. Archaeologists have found that the Roman roads were usually so well constructed that later roads were built right over them. Just under the asphalt of the modern road, which runs parallel to the Wadi Kelt near the Monastery of St. George Hodzeva, is the old Roman road that our Lord walked on from Jerusalem to Jericho.

The original monastery, built in the early 5th century by five Syrian hermits, was limited to the church of St. Stephen the Protomartyr with several cave cells around it. In the second half of the 5th century, St. John of Hodzeva transformed the monastery into a lavra-cenobium, leaving certain cells for the anchorites, but instituting areas for communal living also. It was in this monastery that St. George of Hodzeva spent most of his monastic life, eventually becoming abbot and enlarging the monastery greatly. Both sides of the Wadi Kelt were honeycombed with caves of the solitary monks, and a large church and other buildings were built out of the side of the cliff. The Persian invaders slew some 4,000 of the monastery's 5,000 monks, dispersed the remainder, and destroyed the monastery buildings. A few monks reassembled, making it possible for the

The cave where the Prophet Elias stayed and was fed by the raven during the drought in Israel. St. Joachim also prayed here that he might be deemed worthy to have a child.

monastery to survive until the 12th century, when it was rebuilt by the Emperor Manuel I Comnenus. The monastery was abandoned in the 13th century until restorations began in 1878.

It is wise to begin the descent to the monastery in the early morning, since the sun warms the area quickly. Note the aqueduct that runs along the southern side of the Wadi Kelt, carrying water from the Spring of St. Hariton (situated closer to Jerusalem) to Jericho.

From the courtyard of the monastery one can see the rows of holes that contained the floor joists and, faintly, the frescoes that had adorned the church built by St. George. Inside the monastery, the present catholicon is dedicated to the Nativity of the Mother of God. Along the left wall are relics of the founders of the original monastery; portions of a 6th century mosaic floor can also be seen. Behind this church is the chapel of St. Stephen the Protomartyr which contains the relics of St. George of Hodzeva, the incorrupt relics of Fr. John the Romanian, the skulls of several of the fathers that were martyred by the Persians, and many other relics.

Father John the Romanian was a zealot for Orthodoxy who lived in one of the caves in the areas called "the Skete of St. Anne" (further towards Jericho along the Wadi Kelt). He died in 1960 at the age of 48 after a life of harsh asceticism. His relics were brought to the monastery from his cave in 1980.

On the monastery's third level is the cave of the Prophet Elias and St. Joachim. During the reign of King Ahab, the Prophet Elias prophesied that because the children of Israel had turned from God to worshipping idols, "there shall not be dew or rain these years, but according to my word" (I Kings 17:1). During the drought he stayed in this cave, drinking water from the brook below and being fed twice daily by ravens. By nature, ravens are so uncompassionate that they ignore the needs of their own young. The holy Fathers of the Church comment that God chose ravens to feed His Prophet in order to stir some compassion within him for the people that were dying of thirst because of his zeal. When the brook dried up, God sent him to the widow of Serapta to be fed.

In the days of St. Joachim, the father of the Mother of God, this cave was a place of pilgrimage. Grieving over his childlessness after his sacrifice was not accepted at the Temple, St. Joachim journeyed here and prayed ardently for a child. St. Anna, informed of what had transpired in Jerusalem, prayed at home. The Archangel Gabriel appeared to each of them and announced that their prayers had been heard and that they would have a child. Some sources state that after the Mother of God was brought to the Temple, St. Anna lived in asceticsim in the area of the ravine that bears her name.

Dismissal Troparion of St. George of Hodzeva
Plagal of First Tone (5th)

Having cultivated the word of grace, O Father, thou didst reap the illustrious harvest of righteousness as one that had chosen the life of godliness. Wherefore, thou didst prove to be a partaker of the glory of Christ, O God-bearing George. Do thou intercede with Him unceasingly that He have mercy on our souls.

✠

Jericho

One of the oldest cities in the world, Jericho is also the lowest inhabited point on earth. Its fertile soil and abundant water make this truly an oasis in the desert, with many fruit and vegetable groves, wild flowers, and palm trees. The climate is dry and warm, making it a favorite winter retreat for many rulers. This city was the first view of the Promised Land for Jesus of Navi (Joshua) and the Israelites, and the first to be destroyed by them (Joshua 6:1-21). Since it was built at the junction of the main roads, our Saviour passed through Jericho many times in His travels, healing the blind Bartimaeus (St. Luke 18:35-43), visiting with Zacchaeus (St. Luke 19:1-10), and healing the two blind men (St. Matthew 20:29-34).

THE MOUNT OF TEMPTATION

St. Luke 4:1-14

At that time, Jesus being full of the Holy Spirit returned from Jordan, and was led by the Spirit into the wilderness, being forty days tempted of the devil. And in those days He did eat nothing: and when they were ended, He afterward hungered. And the devil said unto Him, If Thou be the Son of God, command this stone that it be made bread. And Jesus answered him, saying, It is written, That man shall not live by bread alone, but by every word of God. And the devil, taking Him up into an high mountain, shewed unto Him all the kingdoms of the world in a moment of time. And the devil said unto Him, All this power will I give Thee, and the glory of them: for that is delivered unto me; and to whomsoever I will I give it. If Thou therefore wilt worship me, all shall be Thine. And Jesus answered and said unto him, Get thee behind Me, Satan: for it is written, Thou shalt worship the Lord thy God, and Him only shalt thou serve. And he brought Him to Jerusalem, and set Him on a pinnacle of the temple, and said unto Him, If Thou be the Son of God, cast Thyself down from hence: for it is written, He shall give His Angels charge over thee, to keep thee: And in their hands they shall bear thee up, lest at any time thou dash thy foot against a stone. And Jesus answering said unto him, It is said, Thou shalt not tempt the Lord thy God. And when the devil had ended all the temptation, he departed from Him for a season. And Jesus returned in the power of the Spirit into Galilee: and there went out a fame of Him through all the region round about.

The Mount of Temptation, also known as Quarantal (*Sarandarion Oros* in Greek), or 40-Day Mountain, is the site where our Saviour was tried by Satan. Here, after spending forty days in prayer and fasting after His baptism, He overcame man's three greatest temptations: that of bodily pleasure, that of wealth, and that of pride (the flesh, the world, and the devil).

A certain monk living on this mountain was greatly tempted to go to Mount Sinai to find peace. As he was preparing to leave, an Angel appeared to him and revealed that our Saviour had remained here in a cave. The monk stayed, but the actual site of our Lord's struggles has been lost.

From this mountain one can see the Jericho Valley, the Dead Sea, the northern Judean desert, and the Jerusalem mountains. In 68 AD the Romans destroyed a Hasmonean-Herodian fortress that had been

The Mount of Temptation. Though difficult to distinguish, the monastery is situated on the left side of the mountain.

built on the summit. In the 4th century St. Hariton founded one of his monasteries here, naming it Douka. Douka served the needs of the hermits living in the many caves on the slope of the mountain until it was destroyed in the 7th century by the Persians. The solitaries were scattered and, except for a brief period of occupation during the Crusader rule, the mountain remained virtually uninhabited until the late 19th century when the present monastery was built halfway up the slope. At the same time that the monastery was built, a church and hostel were begun at the summit with Russian funds. The Bolshevik Revolution in 1917 cut off the supply of funds, causing the project to be abandoned. The monastery has incorporated many caves into its construction; the rest of the structures jut out from the sheer rock wall of the mountain, giving the illusion that they grew there. An elaborate system collects rainwater for the needs of the monastery.

Some sources state that our Saviour sat on the stone now under the Holy Table during His first temptation.

The catholicon is dedicated to the Annunciation of the Mother God. On ascending a small staircase to the right of the iconostasis, one finds a small chapel. Some sources state that our Saviour sat on the stone, which is now located under the Holy Table and prayed during the time of His first temptation.

THE SPRING OF THE PROPHET ELISSEUS

Situated near the ruins of ancient Jericho (now called Tell Sultan), which are currently undergoing excavation, the Spring of Elisseus provides water for the whole region via a system of irrigation canals. After he received a double portion of Elias' spirit, Elisseus was approached by the citizens of Jericho, who told him that their water source was noxious. He healed the spring by throwing salt into it (II Kings 2:19-22).

The Spring of the Prophet Elisseus serves as a source of water for the whole region.

THE CHURCH OF THE PROPHET ELISSEUS

St. Luke 19:1-10

In those days, Jesus entered and passed through Jericho. And, behold, there was a man named Zacchæus, which was the chief among the publicans, and he was rich. And he sought to see Jesus who He was; and could not for the press, because he was little of stature. And he ran before, and climbed up into a sycamore tree to see Him: for He was to pass that way. And when Jesus came to the place, He looked up, and saw him, and said unto him, Zacchæus, make haste, and come down; for to day I must abide at thy house. And he made haste, and came down, and received Him joyfully. And when they saw it, they all murmured, saying, That He was gone to be guest with a man that is a sinner. And Zacchæus stood, and said unto the Lord; Behold, Lord, the half of my goods I give to the poor; and if I have taken any thing from any man by false accusation, I restore him fourfold. And Jesus said unto him, This day is salvation come to this house, forsomuch as he also is a son of Abraham. For the Son of man is come to seek and to save that which was lost.

Before the Persian invasion and subsequent domination of the Holy Land, many churches existed in Jericho. When Christians were able to rebuild churches many centuries later, they had lost the location of certain sites. The property on which the Church of the Prophet Elisseus now stands was purchased because of a tradition that somewhere in that area a shrine dedicated to St. Zacchaeus had once existed. After the building of the church was completed, some mosaics with inscriptions were found on a neighboring property bought by the Russian Ecclesiastical Mission, but the area has not been excavated due to the lack of funds. As a commemorative gesture, an old sycamore tree and an icon of our Saviour with St. Zacchaeus have been enshrined on the left side of the church courtyard.

THE MONASTERY OF ST. GERASIMUS

To the southeast of the Jericho Valley, a lone structure can be seen on the barren plane, the Monastery of St. Gerasimus of the Jordan. In the mid-5th century St. Gerasimus founded a large monastery in which both cenobitic and anchoritic monasticism were combined. Those who had recently left the world received monastic training while living in the cenobium, but those who were advanced in the monastic life were permitted to live as anchorites. The monks under St. Gerasimus' care followed his example of non-possessiveness and strict abstinence. For himself, the Saint had the custom of abstaining from all food during Great Lent, partaking only of Holy Communion.

Of his many virtues, St. Gerasimus was perhaps best known for his humility and guilelessness. Once he was led astray into the monophysite heresy, along with many other monastics and laity in the Holy Land; but when St. Euthymius explained to him the error of the heresy, he humbly accepted the correction and rejected the false doctrine of the monophysites.

Once the Saint went to the Jordan to fetch some water and met a lion with a thorn in its paw. After St. Gerasimus extracted the thorn, the lion would not be separated from him. St. Gerasimus named him Jordan. Jordan was given the responsibility for tending the monastery's donkey while it grazed and bringing it to the river for water for the monastery. A passing caravan stole the donkey while the lion was sleeping, and the lion returned in shame to the Saint. Scolding him for supposedly having eaten the donkey, the Saint had Jordan do all the tasks that the donkey had done. When the caravan returned, Jordan recognized the donkey. He took the lead animal's halter in his teeth and led the caravan to the monastery, thus exonerating himself. St. Gerasimus reposed while Jordan was away from the monastery for a few days. Upon his return, Jordan searched for his friend, and the fathers took him to the grave of the Saint. Mourning his loss, Jordan stayed at the grave, refusing to eat, and died after three days.

In the 6th century the fame of this monastery attracted St. Zosimas, an experienced monk of Tyre, and he settled there. During one of the customary retreats into the desert during Great Lent, he was vouchsafed to meet St. Mary of Egypt. The next year he gave her Holy Communion at the Jordan, and the following year he buried her in the desert where he first encountered her.

St. Gerasimus' monastery was destroyed by the Persians and rebuilt and inhabited for a short period of time in the 9th century. When the present fort-like monastery was built in the 19th century, the site of the ancient monastery had already been lost. The present monastery was built over the ruins of the ancient Lavra of Calamon, where St. Sabbas lived before founding his own Lavra. The Lavra of Calamon withstood the attacks of the Persians and served as a fortified refuge for hermits from the surrounding area until the 13th century when it was finally abandoned.

Dismissal Troparion of St. Gerasimus of the Jordan
First Tone

Thou wast shown forth as a dweller of the desert, a summit of ascetics, and a reflection of the angelic life; and thou wast made illustrious by the light of the Spirit, O Gerasimus, blest adornment of the righteous. Wherefore, thou dost unfailingly heal them that cry out to thee with faith: Glory to Him that hath given thee strength. Glory to Him that hath crowned thee. Glory to Him that worketh healings for all through thee.

The Dead Sea

Lying some 3,780 feet (1,100 m) lower than Jerusalem, the Dead Sea is the lowest point on earth, 1,298 feet (396 m) below sea level. It has a salt content approximately ten times that of the Mediterranean and nothing lives in the water; those wishing to swim will find that they cannot sink. The high mineral content of the water makes it therapeutic for many as a bath, but the water is undrinkable, with a distinct sulfur smell and a soapy feel. The Jordan River empties into the Dead Sea, as does the run-off from the neighboring mountain ranges. But due to a very high evaporation rate, and especially the mining activity of the Israelis, the Dead Sea is getting lower every year. Several minerals are already being mined from the water with plans for further expansion.

EN GEDI

Travelling along the desolate western shore of the Dead Sea, one comes to the lush oasis of En Gedi, "Fountain of the Kids." This oasis belonged to the tribe of Judah and was an important stronghold in the desert. En Gedi was first settled in the 7th century BC, and became the center for the production of balsam and the cultivation of rare spices and dates. This is where the Prophet David sought refuge from the wrath of Saul. When Saul was pursuing him and paused to sleep in a cave, the Prophet cut off a piece of Saul's robe, thus testifying to his fidelity (I Samuel 24).

If pilgrims wish to view some of the beautiful flora and fauna, as well as a spectacular 590 foot (180 m) waterfall, there is a national park at En Gedi with an information center at the entrance. A resort on the shore of the Dead Sea offers accommodations and accessibility to the Dead Sea for those wishing to bathe in its waters or to avail themselves of the mineral-rich mud treatments.

Samaria

For ye have planted vineyards on the mountains of Samaria:
plant ye, and praise. (Jeremias 38:5)

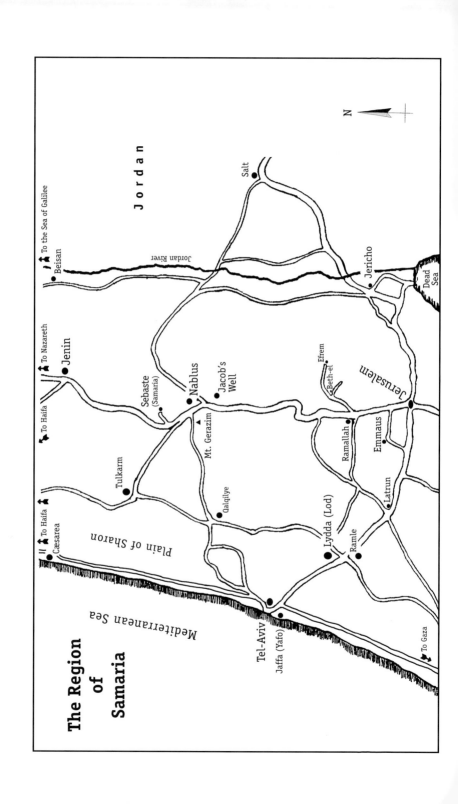

The Region of Samaria

Samaria, the central region of the Holy Land, is bordered by the region of Galilee on the north and the region of Judea on the south. The Prophet King David united the twelve tribes of Israel into one kingdom and gave it into the hands of his son Solomon. After the death of King Solomon in 931 BC, the kingdom was divided into two parts, Judea and Israel. Jerusalem remained the capital of Judea; the capital of Israel was established at Shechem. Omri, the sixth king of Israel (880-871 BC), moved the capital of Israel to the city of Shomrom (translated "Samaria" in the Septuagint).

In 721 BC the Assyrians defeated Hosea, the last king of Israel, destroyed the city of Samaria, and deported its leading citizens to Babylon. The conquerors then imported exiles from other parts of the Assyrian Empire. These newcomers, who eventually intermarried with the remaining Israelites, accepted elements of the Jewish religion and combined them with pagan beliefs. This resulted in a people with mixed lineage and religion called the Samaritans. The Israelites of Judea considered the Samaritans foreigners and heretics. Consequently, they separated themselves from the Samaritans, creating a division that is still in existence. The Samaritans built their own temple on Mount Gerasim and began to worship there. Samaria and the neighboring city of Shechem became the centers of the Samaritan people, whose descendants live there to this day.

The name "Samaria" was also given to the whole of central Palestine from the time of Cyrus, the Persian ruler who permitted the Hebrews to return to their homeland from their captivity in Babylon (539 BC). Many events in the Old Testament were associated with the region of Samaria, including: Abraham's first stop in Canaan where he built an altar (Genesis 12:6-7), Patriarch Jacob's sons' massacre of the inhabitants of Shalem to defend the honor of their sister (Genesis 33:18-35:4), Joseph's burial after the Israelites brought his bones out of Egypt (Joshua 24:32), Joshua's final exhortations to the tribes of Israel (Joshua 24), and Elias' challenge to the priests of Baal to sacrifice without fire on Mount Carmel and the subsequent slaughter of the priests (I Kings 17:1-18:40).

In the New Testament, our Saviour often travelled through the region of Samaria on His way to and from the region of Galilee. In Samaria our Saviour healed the ten lepers (St. Luke 17:11-19) and spoke with St. Photini at the well of Jacob (John 4:5-42). After St. Stephen was stoned, St. Philip preached in Samaria. He converted so many to the Faith that St. Peter and St. John joined him in preaching to the Samaritans (Acts 8:5-25).

Nablus

The present-day city of Nablus was founded in AD 72 by Emperor Vespasian on the site of a Samaritan village which was near the Biblical Shechem. Vespasian called his city Flavia Neapolis and embellished it with Roman temples, colonnaded streets, and a very large Roman theatre. It was in this pagan city that the holy Martyr Justin the Philosopher was born the in the mid-second century. Christianity became established and by the year 314 the Christian community was so large that they had their own bishop.

At the time of the Arab conquest, the city's name was corrupted to Nablus. The Crusaders captured Nablus and made it a royal city with a palace and a citadel. In the ensuing centuries, the city never possessed a powerful status, but neither did it decline. In the mid-19th century, Nablus began to grow; several institutions were built and new neighborhoods sprang up. Relief funds after an earthquake in 1927 aided the rebuilding of many of the old houses and the construction of new ones. At present, Nablus is the largest urban center in Samaria.

JACOB'S WELL

St. John 4:5-42

At that time, Jesus cometh to a city of Samaria, which is called Sychar, near to the parcel of ground that Jacob gave to his son Joseph. Now Jacob's well was there. Jesus therefore, being wearied with His journey, sat thus on the well: and it was about the sixth hour. There cometh a woman of Samaria to draw water: Jesus saith unto her, Give Me to drink. (For His disciples were gone away unto the city to buy meat.) Then saith the woman of Samaria unto Him, How is it that Thou, being a Jew, askest drink of me, which am a woman of Samaria? for the Jews have no dealings with the Samaritans. Jesus answered and said unto her, If thou knewest the gift of God, and Who it is that saith to thee, Give Me to drink; thou wouldest have asked of Him, and He would have given thee living water. The woman saith unto Him, Sir, Thou hast nothing to draw with, and the well is deep: from whence then hast Thou that living water? Art Thou greater than our father Jacob, which gave us the well, and drank thereof himself, and his children, and his cattle? Jesus answered and said unto her, Whosoever drinketh of this water shall thirst again: But whosoever drinketh of the water that I shall give him shall never thirst; but the water that I shall give him shall be in him a well of water springing up into everlasting life. The woman saith unto Him, Sir, give me this water, that I thirst not, neither come hither to draw. Jesus saith unto her, Go, call thy husband, and come hither. The woman answered and said, I have no husband. Jesus said unto her, Thou hast well said, I have no husband: For thou hast had five husbands; and he whom thou now hast is not thy husband: in that saidst thou truly. The woman saith unto Him, Sir, I perceive that Thou art a Prophet. Our fathers worshipped in this mountain; and ye say that in Jerusalem is the place where men ought to worship. Jesus saith unto her, Woman, believe me, the hour cometh, when ye shall neither in this mountain, nor yet at Jerusalem, worship the Father. Ye worship ye know not what: we know what we worship: for salvation is of the Jews. But the hour cometh, and now is, when the true worshippers shall worship the Father in spirit and in truth: for the Father seeketh such to worship Him. God is spirit: and they that worship Him must worship Him in spirit and in truth. The woman saith unto Him, I know that Messias cometh, which is called Christ: when He is come, He will tell us all things. Jesus saith unto her, I that speak unto thee am He. And upon this came His disciples, and marvelled that He talked with the woman: yet no man said, What seekest Thou? or, Why talkest Thou with her? The woman then left her waterpot, and went her way into the city, and saith to the men, Come, see a man, which told me all things that ever I did: is not this the Christ? Then they went out of the city, and came unto Him. In the mean while His disciples prayed Him, saying, Master, eat. But He said unto them, I have meat to eat that ye know not of. Therefore said the disciples one to another, Hath any man brought Him ought to eat? Jesus saith unto them, My meat is to do the will of Him that sent Me, and to finish His work. Say not ye, There are yet four months, and then cometh harvest? behold, I say unto you, Lift up your eyes, and look on the fields; for they are white already to harvest. And he that reapeth receiveth wages, and gathereth fruit unto life eternal: that both he that soweth and he that reapeth may rejoice together. And herein is that saying true, One soweth, and another reapeth. I sent you to reap that whereon ye bestowed no labour: other men laboured, and ye are entered into their labours. And many of the Samaritans of that city believed on Him for the saying of the woman, which testified, He told me all that ever I did. So when the Samaritans were come unto Him, they besought Him that He would tarry with them: and He abode there two days. And many more believed because of His own word; and said unto the woman, Now we believe, not because of thy saying: for we have heard Him ourselves, and know that this is indeed the Christ, the Saviour of the world.

Crypt church at Jacob's Well where our Lord met the Samaritan Woman, St. Photini, commemorated on the Fourth Sunday after Pascha.

After Patriarch Jacob departed with his family and flocks from his father-in-law, Laban, and was reconciled to his brother Esau, he "came to Shalem, a city of Shechem, which is in the land of Canaan… and he bought a parcel of a field, where he had spread his tent, at the hand of the children of Hamor" (Genesis 33:18-19). Jacob dug a deep well here and gave it to his beloved son, Joseph the All-Comely. For centuries this well has been the only well in the area. It was here that one of the greatest revelations in the New Testament, that "God is Spirit," was made to a sinful woman. The holy Fathers of the Church say that it was no coincidence that the time of this meeting was at the same time of day when Eve was tempted. Our Saviour sat on the edge of the well and spoke with the woman, gently revealing her hidden sins. She was moved and gathered the townspeople to hear His words. She and her whole household were baptized and she took the name Photini. They preached the Gospel in Africa and later went to Rome where they were martyred.

The first church at Jacob's Well was a cruciform Byzantine-style church built in the 5th century. It was burned during a revolt of the Samaritans in 485. The church was then rebuilt in the 6th century,

The apse of the unfinished church at Jacob's Well. The two small huts are entrances to the crypt church containing the well.

and in the 12th century, the Crusaders constructed a large church over the well. The lip of the well where our Saviour sat was taken to Constantinople as a blessing for the city, but the well itself has remained the same. Located in a crypt in the middle of a large, unfinished church, it reaches an unusual depth, 120 feet or 40 meters. The church was begun in 1914 with Russian contributions, but work on it was soon abandoned because of the lack of funding due to the Bolshevik Revolution in 1917. Recently, the present guardian of the shrine, Archimandrite Justin, resumed the process of building the church with donations from pilgrims.

Because this well belonged to the Patriarch Jacob, many Jews feel that they should have possession of the shrine. The tension has become so great that several caretakers have been attacked and one, Fr. Philoumenos, was killed by a fanatical American Jew in 1979.

Kontakion of the Sunday of the Samaritan Woman
Plagal of Fourth Tone (8ʰ)

Having come to the well in faith, the Samaritan woman beheld Thee, the Water of Wisdom, whereof having drunk abundantly, she, the renowned one, inherited the Kingdom on high forever.

✠

Sebaste

THE PRISON OF ST. JOHN THE BAPTIST

Mark 6:14-29

And it came to pass that King Herod heard of Him; (for His name was spread abroad;) and he said, That John the Baptist was risen from the dead, and therefore mighty works do shew forth themselves in Him. Others said, That it is Elias. And others said, That it is a prophet, or as one of the prophets. But when Herod heard thereof, he said, it is John, whom I beheaded: he is risen from the dead. For Herod himself had sent forth and laid hold upon John, and bound him in prison for Herodias' sake, his brother Philip's wife: for he had married her. For John had said unto Herod, It is not lawful for thee to have thy brother's wife. Therefore, Herodias had a quarrel against him, and would have killed him; but she could not: for Herod feared John, knowing that he was a just man and holy, and observed him; and when he heard him, he did many things, and heard him gladly. And when a convenient day was come, that Herod on his birthday made a supper to his lords, high captains and chief estates of Galilee; and when the daughter of the said Herodias came in, and danced, and pleased Herod and them that sat with him, the king said unto the damsel, Ask of me whatsoever thou wilt, and I will give it thee. And he sware unto her, Whatsoever thou shalt ask of me, I will give it thee, unto the half of my kingdom. And she went forth, and said unto her mother, What shall I ask? And she said, The head of John the Baptist. And she came in straightway with haste unto the king, and asked saying, I will that thou give me by and by in a charger the head of John the Baptist. And the king was exceeding sorry; yet for his oath's sake, and for their sakes which sat with him, he would not reject her. And immediately the king sent an executioner, and commanded his head to be brought: and he went and beheaded him in the prison, and brought his head in a charger, and gave it to the damsel: and the damsel gave it to her mother. And when his disciples heard of it, they came and took up his corpse, and laid it in a tomb. And the apostles gathered themselves together unto Jesus, and told Him all things, both what they had done, and what they had taught.

In the 9th century BC, King Omri's son, Ahab, married Jezebel and rebuilt the city of Samaria which was located on a high hill. Their luxurious and iniquitous way of life, combined with their idolatrous beliefs, aroused the wrath of the prophets of Israel, especially that of Elias (I Kings 17). The Assyrians destroyed Samaria and carried off many of its citizens to Babylon in 721 BC. In 332 BC, Alexander the Great conquered the city of Samaria and it was razed by the Hasmonean King Jannaeus in 108 BC. In 30 BC the Emperor Augustus presented it to Herod the Great, who rebuilt the city, naming it Sebaste ("Augustus") in honor of the emperor. Herod created a Roman city with a theater, stadium, and forum; and he crowned its citadel with a temple to Augustus.

It was in this city that Herodias gave the birthday party for Herod Antipas where Salome danced and received the venerable head of the Forerunner as wages. St. John's disciples buried their master's body in Sebaste. Fourth century pilgrims described venerating the tombs of the Baptist, Prophet Elisseus, and Prophet Obadiah in a certain shrine, and noted that it was a site of many miracles. By this time Sebaste was already home to a sizeable Christian community. Its bishop, Marinus, attended the First Ecumenical Council in Nicea.

In AD 361 the pagans of Sebaste rioted and desecrated the tombs of the Saints. The Emperor, Julian the Apostate, expressed his approval of their sacrilegious actions. Christians gathered the relics that had been scattered and the veneration of the shrine continued. The city began to decline after the Moslem Arab conquest and this decline continued throughout the following centuries. The shrine was rebuilt by the Crusaders in the 12th century, but in 1187 the cathedral over the shrine was converted into a mosque.

Today Sebaste is only a small village with a few hundred inhabitants, not far from Nablus. Ancient Sebaste is mostly ruins. In 1932 archaeologists unearthed the remains of a small basilica on the summit of the hill. Built in the 5th-6th century, the basilica had a mosaic floor of which some portions remain. In a chapel in the crypt at the eastern end of the northern aisle are some frescoes with Angels holding the head of St. John the Baptist. This crypt is thought by some to be the prison cell where St. John was beheaded. Others speculate that it is the site of one of the findings of the head of the Forerunner, perhaps where Herodias first buried it. Pilgrim accounts from after the 6th century mention a monastery on the site. The church was rebuilt in the 11th century and a round dome supported by four granite columns was added. Three of the columns are still standing; one has fallen. This church was rebuilt again by the Crusaders, probably in the second half of the 12th century.

The western wall of the ruins of the basilica in Sebaste. The apse in the eastern wall of the basilicia can be seen through the intact inner doorway.

These ruins were recently acquired by the Patriarchate of Jerusalem through Archimandrite Justin, the guardian of Jacob's Well. Once a year, on the Feast of the Beheading of St. John, the few Christians from the village assemble and serve the Liturgy in the ruins. A portable Holy Table is placed where the original Holy Table once was. On one occasion during the service the priest sensed a strong fragrance coming from the ground under the Holy Table. They excavated and found the consecrating relics of the original Holy Table

114

in a silver box, on which was engraved, "A piece of the skull of St. John the Forerunner and Baptist."

Pilgrims wishing to venerate this ancient Christian shrine should contact Archimandrite Justin at Jacob's Well.

In the eastern wall of the crypt is an apse with an attached Holy Table under which the fresco of Angels holding the head of the Forerunner is discernible. The crypt is thought by some to be the place where St. John the Baptist was beheaded; others consider it to be one of the sites where his head was found.

Dismissal Troparion of the Forerunner
Second Tone

The memory of the just is celebrated with hymns of praise, but the Lord's testimony is sufficient for thee, O Forerunner; for thou hast proved to be truly even more venerable than the Prophets, since thou wast granted to baptize in the running waters Him Whom they proclaimed. Wherefore, having contested for the truth, thou didst rejoice to announce the good tidings even to those in Hades: that God hath appeared in the flesh, taking away the sin of the world and granting us great mercy.

✠

Galilee

Act quickly, O land of Zebulon, land of Nephthalim, and the rest inhabiting the sea-coast, and the land beyond Jordan, Galilee of the Gentiles. O people walking in darkness, behold a great light; ye that dwell in the region and shadow of death, a light shall shine upon you. (Esaias 9:1-2)

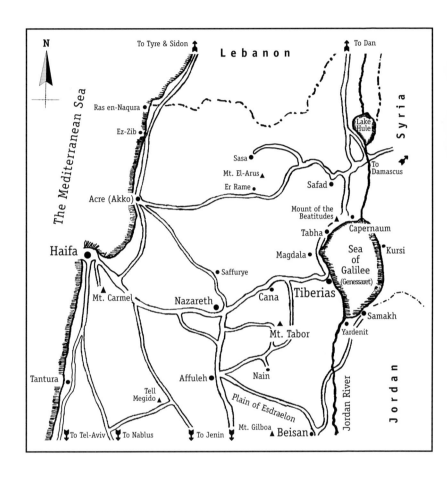

The Region of Galilee

Moujnt Tabor

St. Matthew 17:1-9

At that time, Jesus taketh Peter, James, and John his brother, and bringeth them up into a high mountain apart, and was transfigured before them: and His face did shine as the sun, and His raiment was white as the light. And behold, there appeared unto them Moses and Elias talking with Him. Then answered Peter, and said unto Jesus, Lord, it is good for us to be here: if Thou wilt, let us make here three tabernacles; one for Thee, and one for Moses, and one for Elias. While he yet spake, behold, a bright cloud overshadowed them: and behold, a voice out of the cloud, which said, This is My beloved Son, in Whom I am well pleased; hear ye Him. And when the disciples heard it, they fell on their face, and were sore afraid. And Jesus came and touched them, and said, Arise and be not afraid. And when they had lifted up their eyes, they saw no man, save Jesus only. And as they came down from the mountain, Jesus charged them, saying, Tell the vision to no man, until the Son of man be risen again from the dead.

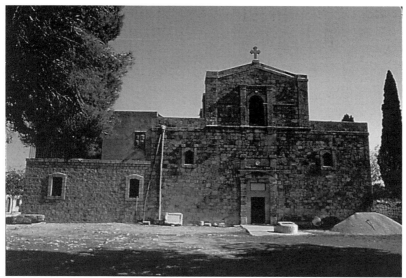

The Orthodox Church of the Transfiguration on Mount Tabor.

119

The traditional site of our Saviour's Transfiguration, Mount Tabor is an isolated dome-shaped mountain in eastern lower Galilee. It has been a site of Christian worship from the earliest times, following the example of our Lord Who "went up into [this] mountain to pray" (St. Luke 9:28). A web of catacombs recently discovered under the courtyard and church of the Orthodox contains a chapel with a 3rd-century Holy Table and other important artifacts. Archaeologists surmise that these caves also served as a hiding place during persecutions. In the 4th century a church was built on Mount Tabor, and

Interior of the Church of the Transfiguration, built in the 19th century.

two more were built in the 5th century. Pilgrims and monastics flocked to the hallowed mountain, and over the centuries several small monasteries existed at the summit. When the Moslems recaptured the area in the 13th century, they destroyed all the Christian buildings and built a fortress over some of the ruins. In the mid-19th century Christians were permitted to rebuild. On the northern section of the summit the Roman Catholics built a monastery, and later,

Holy Table from the 3rd century in the catacombs on Mount Tabor.

a hostel and Byzantine-style basilica. In 1862, on the southern portion of the summit, the Orthodox built a monastery, a large church dedicated to the Transfiguration, and a chapel dedicated to Melchisedek, the King of Salem.

Early pilgrims hiked up 4,300 steps carved into the rock, but now access to the summit is via a very steep and winding road which is only accessible to small vehicles. A taxi service is available at the parking lot at the foot of the mountain. Pilgrims should specify to the driver that they wish to visit the Orthodox church, not the Roman Catholic shrine.

☦

Dismissal Troparion of the Transfiguration
Grave Tone (7th)

Thou wast transfigured on the mountain, O Christ our God, showing to Thy disciples Thy glory as each one could endure. Shine forth Thou on us who are sinners all Thy light ever unending, through the prayers of the Theotokos; Light-bestower, glory to Thee.

☦

121

Nazareth

St. Luke 1:24-38

In those days Elisabeth, the wife of Zacharias, conceived, and hid herself five months, saying, Thus hath the Lord dealt with me in the days wherein He looked on me, to take away my reproach among men. And in the sixth month the Angel Gabriel was sent from God unto a city of Galilee, named Nazareth, to a virgin espoused to a man whose name was Joseph, of the house of David; and the virgin's name was Mary. And the Angel came in unto her, and said, Rejoice, thou full of grace, the Lord is with thee: blessed art thou among women. And when she saw him, she was troubled at his saying, and cast in her mind what manner of salutation this should be. And the Angel said unto her, Fear not, Mary: for thou hast found favour with God. And, behold, thou shalt conceive in thy womb, and bring forth a son, and shalt call His name JESUS. He shall be great, and shall be called the Son of the Most High: and the Lord God shall give unto Him the throne of His father David: And He shall reign over the house of Jacob for ever; and of His kingdom there shall be no end. Then said Mary unto the Angel, How shall this be, seeing I know not a man? And the Angel answered and said unto her, The Holy Spirit shall come upon thee, and the power of the Most High shall overshadow thee: therefore also that holy one which shall be born of thee shall be called the Son of God. And, behold, thy cousin Elisabeth, she hath also conceived a son in her old age: and this is the sixth month with her, who was called barren. For with God nothing shall be impossible. And Mary said, Behold the handmaid of the Lord; be it unto me according to thy word. And the Angel departed from her.

Tradition states that the Annunciation of the Archangel Gabriel to the Mother of God, "Rejoice, thou full of grace, the Lord is with thee..." (St. Luke 1:28) took place by a spring. That spring is now located in the crypt of the Orthodox church dedicated to the Annunciation in Nazareth. The crypt, decorated with tiles from Armenia, is a remnant of the church the Crusaders erected at the site. The present church above the crypt was built in the 18th century; its iconostasis

The spring where the Archangel Gabriel greeted the Most Holy Theotokos lies in the crypt of the Orthodox Church dedicated to Annunciation in Nazareth.

was donated in 1701 by a Greek merchant. The church has recently been beautifully frescoed in the traditional style by Romanian iconographers. Because the local faithful are Arab Christians, the inscriptions are in Arabic as well as in Greek.

On the right side of the innermost part of the crypt is a set of well-worn stairs used for centuries by the local inhabitants as they came to draw water for their needs. Since this spring is a source of water for the whole village, it is now piped out to the square in front of the church.

Dismissal Troparion of the Annunciation
Fourth Tone

Today is the fountainhead of our salvation and the manifestation of the mystery which was from eternity. The Son of God becometh the Virgin's Son, and Gabriel proclaimeth the good tidings of grace; for this cause, we also cry to the Mother of God with him: Rejoice, thou who art full of grace; the Lord is with thee.

Cana

St. John 2:1-11

At that time, there was a marriage in Cana of Galilee; and the mother of Jesus was there: And both Jesus was called, and His disciples, to the marriage. And when they wanted wine, the mother of Jesus saith unto Him, They have no wine. Jesus saith unto her, Woman, what is that to Me and thee? Mine hour is not yet come. His mother saith unto the servants, Whatsoever He saith unto you, do it. And there were set there six waterpots of stone, after the manner of the purifying of the Jews, containing two or three firkins apiece. Jesus saith unto them, Fill the waterpots with water. And they filled them up to the brim. And He saith unto them, Draw out now, and bear unto the governor of the feast. And they bare it. When the ruler of the feast had tasted the water that was made wine, and knew not whence it was: (but the servants which drew the water knew;) the governor of the feast called the bridegroom, and saith unto him, Every man at the beginning doth set forth good wine; and when men have well drunk, then that which is worse: but thou hast kept the good wine until now. This beginning of miracles did Jesus in Cana of Galilee, and manifested forth His glory; and His disciples believed on Him.

About 5 miles (8 km) northeast of Nazareth is the small village of Cana, the site of the wedding feast in the Gospel of St. John. Here our Saviour's first miracle was performed for the joy of man, that the poverty of the newlyweds would not be a hindrance to the celebration. Tradition says that the groom at the wedding feast was Simon the Zealot, who, after witnessing the miracle, followed our Saviour with special eagerness.

The holy Fathers of the Church say that our Lord's question, "What is that to Me and thee?" has frequently been mistranslated in English as "What have I to do with thee?" Our Saviour reverenced His mother. His words meant, "We did not come to drink wine, so what does it matter?" And yet, in her unhesitating faith, the Mother of God knew that her request would be fulfilled.

The Church of St. George in Cana of Galilee.

The marriage feast is an image often used by our Saviour, the disciples, and the holy Fathers as an image of the Kingdom of Heaven. The Bridegroom is our Saviour and the Bride is every Orthodox Christian.

The Orthodox church in Cana is dedicated to St. George and has two ancient stone waterpots reputed to be of the six original pots that held the water-made-wine. In the late 19th century the church was rebuilt, but due to the lack of funds, the interior was not completed. The newly-wedded Grand Duke Sergei Romanov and his wife, the Grand Duchess Elizabeth, visited the church at the time and were moved to provide money for the iconostasis as well as many church articles for the embellishment of the church. Hence, their patron Saints are depicted on the iconostasis in honor of them and their visit. At the back of the church is a large icon depicting many of the miracles and events that took place in Galilee and its environs — the Annunciation, Transfiguration, Wedding of Cana, Feeding of the 5,000, Beheading of St. John the Baptist, our Saviour's encounter with St. Photini, and the Calming of the Sea of Galilee.

One of the water jugs that contained the water that our Lord turned into wine at the Wedding of Cana.

The Sea of Galilee

In the New Testament the Sea of Galilee was also called the Lake or **Sea of Tiberias**, or the **Lake of Gennesaret**, depending on which shore the speaker was from. The largest freshwater lake in Israel, it is a relatively small body of water (only 12.5 miles (20km) long from north to south and 7.5 miles (12km) wide at its widest point); despite its small size, it is subject to sudden and violent storms. Surrounded by rolling hills where our Saviour preached and worked many miracles, and well-known for its natural beauty and temperate weather, the Sea of Galilee also attracts many tourists.

The Sea of Galilee, also known as the Sea of Tiberias or Lake Gennesaret.

TIBERIAS

On the western shore of the Sea of Galilee is the city of Tiberias, built by Herod at an important crossroads in 18-20 AD and named in honor of the Roman Emperor Tiberius. After the destruction of Jerusalem in 70 AD, Tiberias became a major center of Jewish life. The ruins of ancient synagogues and tombs of famous Jewish sages draw pilgrims from all over the world. After an earthquake leveled the city in 1033, the Crusaders reestablished the city slightly to the north of the original site. At present it is largely a resort town, with hot mineral springs and many tourist attractions.

MAGDALA

Magdala, the city of St. Mary Magdalene, is 4 miles (6 km) north of Tiberias. In our Saviour's time, Magdala was one of the most important cities in the region because of its fishing and textile industries. Recently, several fishing boats from the time of our Saviour have been recovered from the muddy banks of the Sea of Tiberias; one is currently on display in Beit Allon. Some sources state that after our Saviour's Resurrection and St. Mary Magdalene's visit to Caesar, Magdala became a place of pilgrimage, and a church was built on the traditional site of her house. This church was destroyed in the 7th century and rebuilt in the Crusader period, but has remained in ruins since the 13th century. Excavations in Magdala have also uncovered the ruins of an early Byzantine monastery.

TABHA

St. John 6:5-14

When Jesus lifted up His eyes, and saw a great company come unto Him, He saith unto Philip, Whence shall we buy bread, that these may eat? And this He said to prove him: for He Himself knew what He would do. Philip answered Him, Two hundred pennyworth of bread is not sufficient for them, that every one of them may take a little. One of His disciples, Andrew, Simon Peter's brother, saith unto Him, there is a lad here, which hath five barley loaves, and two small fishes: but what are they among so many? And Jesus said, Make the men sit down. Now there was much grass in the place. So the men sat down, in number about five thousand. And Jesus took the loaves; and when He had given thanks, He distributed to the disciples, and the disciples to them that were set down; and likewise of the fishes as much as they would. When they were filled, He said unto His disciples, Gather up the fragments that remain, that nothing be lost. Therefore they gathered them together, and filled twelve baskets with the fragments of the five barley loaves, which remained over and above unto them that had eaten.

Tabha, the traditional location of the multiplication of the loaves by our Saviour (St. John 6:5-14), derives its name from a mispronunciation of *Heptapegon*, meaning "seven springs." This refers to the

A mosaic representation of the five loaves and two fishes that fed the 5,000 is found in the floor near the Holy Table in the apse of a 5th-century basilica. These ruins are now part of a 20th century Benedictine church.

seven springs that flowed in the area, five of which are still active. Excavations at the site have discovered traces of a 4th-century church underneath the more elaborate and complete ruins of a 5th-century basilica. Destroyed by the Persians, the place was abandoned and eventually forgotten until the late 19th century when portions of the mosaic floor were uncovered. Further excavations revealed the mosaic representation of the miracle — a basket of loaves with a fish on either side — in the apse of the altar on the floor behind the Holy

Table. Some sources state that the rock under the Holy Table is where our Lord placed the loaves and fish when He blessed and multiplied them. Also preserved are intricate mosaics of the flora and fauna of the area as well as several inscriptions requesting intercessions for their donors. A large church that incorporated the ruins of the 5th-century basilica was built by Benedictine monks in 1935.

CAPERNAUM

St. Mark 1:21-31

At that time they went into Capernaum; and straightway on the sabbath day Jesus entered into the synagogue, and taught. And they were astonished at His doctrine: for He taught them as one that had authority, and not as the scribes. And there was in their synagogue a man with an unclean spirit; and he cried out, saying, Let us alone; what have we to do with Thee, Thou Jesus of Nazareth? art Thou come to destroy us? I know Thee Who Thou art, the Holy One of God. And Jesus rebuked him, saying, Hold thy peace, and come out of him. And when the unclean spirit had torn him, and cried with a loud voice, he came out of him. And they were all amazed, insomuch that they questioned among themselves, saying, What thing is this? what new doctrine is this? for with authority commandeth He even the unclean spirits, and they do obey Him. And immediately His fame spread abroad throughout all the region round about Galilee. And forthwith, when they were come out of the synagogue, they entered into the house of Simon and Andrew, with James and John. But Simon's wife's mother lay sick of a fever, and anon they tell Him of her. And He came and took her by the hand, and lifted her up; and immediately the fever left her, and she ministered unto them.

Capernaum, the city where our Saviour settled at the beginning of His ministry — "And leaving Nazareth, He came and dwelt in Capernaum, which is upon the seacoast," (St. Matthew 4:13) — is the site of many of His miracles and the home of several of the apostles. In the environs of Capernaum our Saviour cured the demoniac (St. Mark 1:21-28), raised the paralytic (St. Mark 2:1-12), healed St. Peter's mother-in-law (St. Mark 1:29-31), restored the centurion's servant (St. Matthew 8:5-13), healed the woman with an issue of blood, and raised Jairus' daughter from the dead (St. Mark 5:21-43). Built in the 2nd century BC, Capernaum was a small, unfortified, unimportant town. Because of Christ's preaching and His many miracles, large crowds flocked to Capernaum. These formed the nucleus of one of the earliest Christian congregations. During some excavations, the Franciscans uncovered what is thought to be the site of St. Peter's house. The oldest part is from the 1st century BC, and additional structures were added later. In the 5th century, these structures were leveled and an octagonal church with mosaic floor was erected. The Franciscans have built a modern chapel over the remains of this church.

Excavated ruins of the house of the Apostle Peter in Capernaum. A modern chapel has been built over the ruins by the Franciscans.

Near the church of St. Peter are the ruins of a very ornate synagogue built in the late 2nd or early 3rd century. It is thought to have been built on the remains of the synagogue in which our Saviour worshipped, taught, and healed. It is constructed of white limestone, which must have been brought from a distance, as the local stone is black. Its lavish decorations possibly incorporated some

The ruins of a 2nd-century synagogue in Capernaum built on the site of and using materials from the synagogue in which our Saviour taught.

of the carvings from the earlier synagogue, and much of the ornamentation can still be seen. By the 2nd century, Capernaum was a Judeo-Christian community whose inhabitants lived in relative harmony. Capernaum suffered a decline in approximately the 7th century and was finally abandoned in the 8th century.

KURSI – THE LAND OF THE GADARENES

St. Mark 5:1-20

And they came over unto the other side of the sea, into the country of the Gadarenes. And when He was come out of the ship, immediately there met Him out of the tombs a man with an unclean spirit, who had his dwelling among the tombs; and no man could bind him, no, not with chains: because that he had been often bound with fetters and chains, and the chains had been plucked asunder by him, and the fetters broken in pieces: neither could any man tame him. And always, night and day, he was in the mountains, and in the tombs, crying, and cutting himself with stones. But when he saw Jesus afar off, he ran and worshipped Him, and cried with a loud voice, and said, What have I to do with Thee, Jesus, thou Son of the Most High God? I adjure Thee by God, that Thou torment me not. For He said unto him, Come out of the man, thou unclean spirit. And He asked him, What is thy name? And he answered, saying, My name is Legion: for we are many. And he besought Him much that He would not send them away out of the country. Now there was there nigh unto the mountains a great herd of swine feeding. And all the devils besought Him, saying, Send us into the swine, that we may enter into them. And forthwith Jesus gave them leave. And the unclean spirits went out, and entered into the swine: and the herd ran violently down a steep place into the sea, (they were about two thousand;) and were choked in the sea. And they that fed the swine fled, and told it in the city, and in the country. And they went out to see what it was that was done. And they come to Jesus, and see him that was possessed with the devil, and had the legion, sitting, and clothed, and in his right mind: and they were afraid. And they that saw it told them how it befell to him that was possessed with the devil, and also concerning the swine. And they began to pray Him to depart out of their coasts. And when He was come into the ship, he that had been possessed with the devil prayed Him that he might be with Him. Howbeit Jesus suffered him not, but saith unto him, Go home to thy friends, and tell them how great things the Lord hath done for thee, and hath had compassion on thee. And he departed, and began to publish in Decapolis how great things Jesus had done for him.

Kursi, located near the road leading to the Golan Heights on the eastern shore of the sea, is identified as "the country of the Gergesenes" (St. Matthew 8:28-34) or the Gadarenes (St. Luke 8:26-36). Here our Saviour permitted the demons that had possessed one man to enter into a herd of swine feeding close by. The demons caused the herd to run into the sea where they were drowned. The townsfolk asked our Saviour to leave, not in the manner of St. Peter's "depart from me, for I am a sinful man, O Lord" (St. Luke 5:8), but as ones who had already lost much monetary profit and did not intend to lose more. Our Saviour's presence also reminded them that their ways were contrary to the law and they did not wish to change.

In the mid-5th century a large monastery was built on this site. St. Sabbas and his disciples visited it in 491. The church here was a

The restored ruins of the monastery built on the site of the healing of the demoniac in Kursi. St. Sabbas and his disciples visited this monastery in 491.

basilica with a floor covered with colorful mosaics, some of which are well preserved. Under the chapel on the southern side of the main hall is a crypt in which thirty skeletons, presumably those of monks, were buried. In addition to the church, buildings for the monks and pilgrims, workshops, ovens, and courtyards were found in excavations and have been restored. A pillar to the far right of the church is thought to mark the place where the demoniac was healed. Some sources state that the monastery was destroyed in the 8th century by an earthquake and later forgotten.

THE JORDAN RIVER

St. Matthew 3:13-17

At that time cometh Jesus from Galilee to Jordan unto John, to be baptized of him. But John forbad Him, saying, I have need to be baptized of Thee, and comest Thou to me? And Jesus answering said unto him, Suffer it to be so now: for thus it becometh us to fulfil all righteousness.

Then he suffered Him. And Jesus, when He was baptized, went up straightway out of the water: and, lo, the heavens were opened unto Him, and He saw the Spirit of God descending like a dove, and lighting upon Him: and lo a voice from heaven, saying, This is my beloved Son, in whom I am well pleased.

The Jordan River is the most important river in the Holy Land, both as a source of water and because of its association with religious events in both the Old and New Testaments. The Israelites camped on its banks before crossing into the Promised Land (Joshua 3:1), and the water of the Jordan became "as a wall," allowing the

The Jordan River.

people to cross over on dry ground (Joshua 3:13-17). It parted again for the Prophets Elias and Elisseus when the water was smitten with the mantle of Elias (II Kings 2:8-13). The Prophet Elisseus sent Naaman the Syrian to bathe in its waters seven times to cure his leprosy (II Kings 5:10), and by means of a stick, Elisseus retrieved from its waters the axe head that had slipped off its handle (II Kings 6:1-7). On the banks of the Jordan, the Forerunner and Baptist preached repentance and baptized people in its streams (St.

Matthew 3:5-6) and then was vouchsafed to baptize our Lord and God and Saviour Jesus Christ (St. Matthew 3:13-17).

Four streams combine to form the Jordan River, which enters the Sea of Galilee at its northeastern tip and leaves it at its southwestern corner. Called "the Rusher," the Jordan River constantly erodes its banks as it flows toward the Dead Sea. At the time of this writing, the traditional site of our Lord's baptism by St. John the Baptist is inaccessible as it is in a military zone. The Monastery of St. John the Baptist which, by tradition, stood near the site of the Baptism and on the site of the Cave of the Forerunner, has been shelled. This area east of Jericho has also been identified with the ancient Bethabara (Aramaic for "crossing"), the place where the Israelites crossed the Jordan with the Ark. The current here is very strong and the water is often a brown color from all the sediment that it carries.

Pilgrims wishing to immerse themselves in the sanctified waters of the Jordan generally go to **Yardenit**, a place close to where the Jordan leaves the Sea of Galilee. Yardenit offers changing rooms for pilgrims as well as very easy access to the water, since the current is much more gentle here. The traditional attire for Orthodox pilgrims is a long white baptismal robe (hetona) which pilgrims save to be buried in.

Dismissal Troparion of Theophany
First Tone

When Thou wast baptized in the Jordan, O Lord, the worship of the Trinity was made manifest; for the voice of the Father bare witness to Thee, calling Thee His beloved Son. And the Spirit in the form of a dove confirmed the certainty of the word. O Christ our God, Who hast appeared and hast enlightened the world, glory be to Thee.

✠

The
Sinai Peninsula

The chariot host of God is ten thousandfold, yea, thousands of them that abound in number; the Lord is among them at Sinai, in His holy place. (Ps. 67:18)

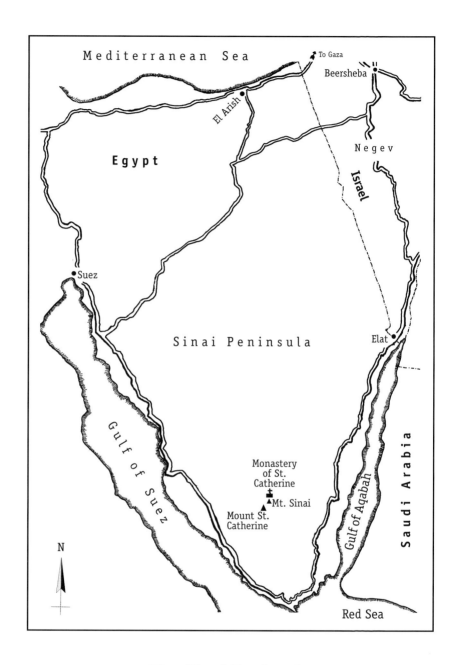

The Sinai Peninsula

Sinai

Stretched between the Gulf of Suez and the Gulf of Aqabah, Sinai is a triangular peninsula, a wilderness of rugged mountains and inhospitable desert. The environment varies greatly with every hour of travel, bringing different temperatures, a variety of atmospheric conditions and soil, and hills of diverse builds and color. The northern part of the peninsula bordering the Mediterranean Sea supports most of the population. Small towns and villages scattered along the coasts benefit from the more stable temperatures and availability of water. The interior, however, with its extremes of temperature and unproductive soil, is home to few other than nomadic Bedouins and monastics.

It was through this "great and terrible wilderness" (Deuteronomy 1:19) that Moses led the chosen people of God from the Red Sea when they fled from Pharaoh. Following a pillar of fire, he led them to Mount Sinai, where he had seen the astonishing miracle of the bush that burned without being consumed and where God had called him to deliver the people from their bondage (Exodus 3:1-12). In Sinai God brought water from a rock to comfort the thirsting people (Exodus 17:1-6). Here Amalek fought with Israel, and God granted victory to Israel when Moses' arms were outstretched in the form of a cross (Exodus 17:8-12). Here God manifested Himself to Moses; he received the revelation of the law and established the priesthood, the sacrifice, and the worship of God in the tabernacle (Exodus 19-40). For the space of forty years the Israelites wandered "in a land barren and untrodden and unwatered" (Psalm 62:1) until the Lord brought them into the Promised Land (Joshua 1). It was here that Elias fled from Jezebel and camped on Mount Horeb, and was granted to hear the voice of the Lord in a gentle breeze (I Kings 19:1-18).

The Monastery of St. Catherine

THE HISTORY OF THE MONASTERY

Since the early 3rd century, Christian hermits desiring to dwell near the God-trodden mountain of Sinai have made their abode in its environs. Several large mountain ranges offered them shelter and, to some extent, protection; and hidden oases supplied them with their physical necessities. In AD 330 St. Helen had a church dedicated to the Mother of God and a modest fort constructed around

The Monastery of St. Catherine at the foot of Mt. Sinai as seen from the mountain opposite.

the site of the Burning Bush. The anchorites would gather in the church on the eves of feast days and Sundays and return to their seclusion after the Liturgy.

Pilgrims began making the strenuous journey to visit the holy sites. The pilgrim Egeria, the same who visited Jerusalem in the late 4th century, also visited Mount Sinai. She writes of a small church on the summit of Mount Sinai, one on Mount Horeb, and a third at the site of the Burning Bush. Because of constant attacks from nomadic marauders, in the 6th century the Emperor Justinian built a monastery dedicated to the Transfiguration of our Lord. It was constructed within a strong fortress, and the monastics formed a cenobium. He also settled a colony of mercenaries nearby to attend to the monastery's protection and needs. These mercenaries intermarried with the local Bedouins, forming the Djebeliye ("Mountaineer") tribe which still serves the monastery.

St. John Climacus, author of *The Ladder of Divine Ascent*, was abbot of the monastery late in the 6th century. He often stood in prayer beneath the great mosaic of the Transfiguration in the apse above the Holy Table. *The Ladder* is a God-inspired book, an invaluable handbook for cenobitic monastics, replete with observations and teachings taken from St. John's long experience as an ascetic and struggler against the passions. Indeed, this sacred book is a classic not only for monastics, but for all Christians concerned about their salvation.

In 640 the Moslems conquered Egypt, including Sinai. The monastery became a Christian island surrounded by Islam and severed from Byzantium. When later iconoclast Byzantine emperors ordered all the icons destroyed, Sinai was cut off from imperial authority, and the Christians there were able to ignore the heretical decrees. Some of the icons protected by the monastery at that time are among the oldest icons in the world today, irreplaceable treasures amid the monastery's collection of over 2,000 icons. Hoping to obtain some security in their vulnerable position, the monks wrote to Mohammed and requested his protection. The request was granted and, in the *Immunity Covenant*, Mohammed instructed his followers to protect the monks of Sinai. Subsequent rulers issued decrees confirming the protected status of the monastery, but in about 1000 AD the Caliph al-Hakim set out to obliterate the monastery. To avert certain destruction, the monks quickly converted a two-story guest house near the church into a mosque, complete with minaret. The monks met the Caliph en route, and convinced him to spare the monastery because it was a holy place for Moslems as well as Christians and had a mosque within its walls.

The Crusades created a resurgence of interest in Mount Sinai and its dependencies among European Christians. After the transfer of some of the relics of St. Catherine to France and the writing of her life by St. Symeon Metaphrastes in the 10th century, the fame of the monastery spread even further, and it was popularly renamed the Monastery of St. Catherine. Monks from all nations were attracted to the monastery, and at times there were whole colonies of Syrian, Georgian, Latin, and Slavic monks.

THE LIFE OF ST. CATHERINE

St. Catherine was born in the late 2nd century, the only daughter of the ruler of Alexandria. She was incomparably beautiful, very learned in all secular wisdom, and exceedingly kind. When she became of age, St. Catherine refused to marry, wishing to preserve her virginity. Her mother, a secret Christian, took Catherine to her own spiritual father for his counsel. He observed Catherine's manner and resolved to bring her to the Faith. He described our Saviour to her and aroused her interest in Him, Whom she thought to be a mere man. Following the elder's instructions, Catherine prayed and was vouchsafed a visitation of the Mother of God and her Son, Who would not look at Catherine. She was told that if she wished to gaze upon the face of the Child, she should return to the elder and follow his instructions. She did so and was catechized thoroughly and baptized. After praying earnestly, she fell asleep and once more beheld the Mother of God and Child, Who, this time, looked benevolently upon her. The Lord gave her a ring as a token of her betrothal to Him and Catherine awoke with the ring on her finger.

When Emperor Maximinus ordered a general assembly and public sacrifice, Catherine grieved greatly over the loss of so many souls and fearlessly went to the temple. Being permitted to speak to the emperor, she quoted the ancient philosophers and proclaimed the error of idolatry with such eloquence that no one was able to refute her. The emperor assembled one hundred fifty scholars to debate with Catherine concerning the Faith. Catherine defeated the rhetoricians and converted them to Christ. The enraged emperor ordered them burned alive, but when the Christians went to gather their relics they found that their bodies were untouched by the flames and they buried them with honor.

After attempting flattery, the emperor resorted to torture and had Catherine scourged severely, then imprisoned. While she was in prison, the emperor's wife, Faustina, and his commander-in-chief, Porphyrius, together with two hundred soldiers visited her and were converted. A wheel of torture was prepared for the Saint, but an Angel freed her and many others were killed instead. When Faustina reproached her husband for his stubbornness in battling God, in a frenzy he ordered her mutilated and beheaded. Porphyrius and his men buried her relics and then appeared before the emperor and proclaimed their faith in Christ. They were also beheaded. The emperor, upset over his losses, attempted with flatteries to convince the Saint to marry him. Unable to do so, he ordered her beheaded outside the city and, instead of blood, milk flowed from her sacred relics. In that hour her relics were translated by Angels to a high mountain near Mount Sinai, now called Mount St. Catherine. Several centuries later, the location of the relics of St. Catherine was revealed in a dream to a monk of the monastery. The monks, with much reverence, brought her precious relics to the monastery.

THE MONASTERY TODAY

The monastery lies in the Wadi ed-Deir ("The Valley of the Monastery") below Mount Sinai. To the west the valley levels out into the Plain of er-Raha where, according to tradition, the Israelites camped while waiting for Moses to return from the mountain. The long approach to the monastery from the main road ends at the western side of the fortress near the modest guest quarters, the monastery bookstore, and gardens surrounded by cypress trees. A small chapel on a mound between the monastery and the Plain of er-Raha is dedicated to the Prophet Aaron. It was here that the golden calf venerated by the Israelites during Moses' long absence on the mountain (Exodus 32:4) is supposed to have stood. The Moslems have constructed a round structure behind the chapel enclosing a tomb venerated by some Moslems as that of Aaron.

The monastery courtyard. To the left of the bell tower, the metal roof of the catholicon can be seen.

In spite of later remodelings and additions, the present fortress differs little from the original. In many places the Byzantine bas-relief carvings of crosses, decorative roundels, and other symbols, as well as strategically placed arrow slits and battlements, can still

146

be seen. In various places large mounds of rubble have been piled against the walls to strengthen them. In the western wall, the present main entrance gate is to the left of the original gate, which, although now walled-up, is still discernible under the flat arch. From the medieval period until the 19th century, all entrances at the ground level were blocked and all supplies, as well as pilgrims, were hauled up in a basket or net through a gate high on the northern wall. At present, only heavy supplies are brought in this manner. Outside the northern wall, near the gate, stands a small chapel dedicated to St. George. The Bedouins, who have great faith in St. George, find that an overnight stay in this chapel often relieves their illnesses.

THE CATHOLICON

After entering the monastery through the low main entrance, one is in an unroofed passage with a view of the church's galvanized iron roof to the northeast. On the right at the base of the wide stone stairs are the church's portals; to the left stands the whitewashed mosque.

The **Gallery of Icons**, located in the narthex of the Catholicon, offers the pilgrim a view of some of the monastery's best-known and unique icons, which form an historic and stylistic progression of Byzantine iconography through the last fifteen centuries. Especially renowned is the 6th century "Sinai Saviour," a nearly life-sized Christ Pantocrator executed in the encaustic technique, an ancient process in which hot wax and pigment are applied to a surface and rubbed in, the colors becoming indelible when cool. In this icon, thought to be inspired by the original Holy Napkin, our Saviour is depicted with a different expression on each side of His face; one side shows tranquility, and the other, concern, portraying the mystery of God incarnate, both divine and human. The icon of St. Peter holding a set of keys is also an ancient encaustic icon; together with the Sinai Saviour, these are among the world's oldest known icons. The narthex and its exterior wooden doors were not part of Justinian's 6th century church. They were built during the time of the Fatimids, 10th to 12th century.

Justinian's large, richly-carved doors connecting the narthex with the nave are made of cedar from Lebanon. They open to reveal the Catholicon, a three-aisled basilica originally dedicated to the Mother of God of the Burning Bush. Several decades after the completion of the church, the magnificent mosaic of the Transfiguration was executed. In the icon of the Holy Transfiguration, Prophets Moses and Elias, who are associated with Mount Sinai and Mount Horeb, are depicted with our Saviour transfigured between them. Their presence at the Transfiguration affirmed that our Saviour is the God of our Fathers, Who had spoken to them, and Whom they had seen in symbols in this holy place. Because of this association, and because of the superb mosaic, the church was officially renamed the "Church of the Transfiguration of Christ the Saviour." After the relics of St. Catherine were brought to the monastery and her life became known in Europe, the monastery was popularly renamed in honor of St. Catherine. The mosaics are intact and were cleaned in 1958 to fully reveal the brilliance of the colors and the masterful technique of the unknown craftsman. Early pilgrims were able to view the entire mosaic of the Transfiguration from the doorway, but the view is currently obstructed by the high 17th century iconostasis and chandeliers. The twelve pillars lining the nave of the church are each hewn from a single piece of local granite. Each pillar bears an icon dating from the 13th century depicting in miniature all the major Saints and feasts of one month, and mounted in each is a reliquary marked with a cross containing relics of Saints celebrated that month.

Originally the ceiling of the church was open. The richly carved beams of the 6th century rafters stood in contrast with the simple but interesting construction of the roof. (The red paint and gold highlights were a later addition.) Three inscriptions requesting prayers for Emperor Justinian, his wife Theodora, and the architect were also visible. In the 18th century, the green panels with star motifs were added to form a continuous ceiling. The original floor was destroyed in the 16th century by raiders searching for hidden treasure, and the present marble and porphyry floor is a stunning display of inlay patterns.

The main Holy Table covering the original marble Holy Table was made in 1675 of inlaid mother of pearl. To the right, under an

18th century marble canopy, are two richly-engraved, silver reliquaries which contain the skull and bejeweled hand of St. Catherine, over which oil lamps burn continuously. Two large reliquaries with relief representations of St. Catherine, gifts from Russia, are kept on either side of the Royal Gates inside the altar.

Along the two side aisles are rows of chapels. On the left, from the rear to the iconostasis, the chapels are dedicated to St. Marina, Sts. Constantine and Helen, and St. Antipas. On the right are the chapels of Sts. Cosmas and Damian, St. Symeon the Stylite, and Sts. Joachim and Anna. On the left side of the iconostasis is an entrance which leads past the sanctuary to a large bronze-sheathed door. Once the door to the Burning Bush courtyard, it is now the entrance to the corner chapel dedicated to St. James the Brother of the Lord. Beyond the small iconostasis within the Chapel of St. James is a door on the right which leads into the Chapel of the Burning Bush.

Dismissal Troparion of St. Catherine the Great Martyr
Plagal of Fourth Tone (8th)
to "Let us worship the Wood"

Let us praise the all-lauded and noble bride of Christ, the godly Catherine, the guardian of Sinai and its defense, who is also our support and succour and our help; for with the Holy Spirit's sword she hath silenced brilliantly the clever among the godless; and being crowned as a Martyr, she now doth ask great mercy for us all.

✠

THE CHAPEL OF THE BURNING BUSH

Exodus 3:2-5

And the Angel of the Lord appeared unto him in a flame of fire out of the midst of a bush: and he looked, and behold, the bush burned with fire and was not consumed…. God called him out of the midst of the bush, and said, Moses, Moses. And he said, Here am I. And He said, Draw not nigh hither: put off thy shoes from off thy feet, for the place whereon thou standest is holy ground.

149

Under the Holy Table in the Burning Bush Chapel is a silver plate marking the original site of the Bush.

In neither St. Helen's nor Justinian's church was there a Burning Bush Chapel; the Bush grew in a small court behind the main apse of the church. A pilgrim writing in 1216 mentions the chapel built of over the roots of the Bush, and that the Bush had been moved outside "or divided among the Christians for relics."

Pilgrims enter the chapel shoeless, in remembrance of God's command to Moses to remove his shoes. The chapel is dedicated to the Annunciation of the Mother of God, as the bush that burnt without being consumed was a foreshadowing of the Virgin who contained the Fire of the Godhead within her womb. Beneath the Holy Table is a marble slab and a silver plate, dated 1696, marking the site the Bush. The tiles covering the walls and apse are striking blue faience from Damascus. This shrine is also held sacred by Moslems.

OTHER SHRINES AROUND THE CATHOLICON

At the back right side of the shrine is another door leading into the other corner chapel dedicated to the Holy Martyred Fathers of

Sinai and Raithu and St. John the Baptist. Relics from the Martyrs have been placed in the wall. From this chapel there is a doorway into the right aisle of the catholicon.

The **Well of Moses**, where the Prophet Moses delivered the daughters of Jethro from the shepherds (Exodus 2:15-19) is located in an alcove north of the catholicon. The very deep natural cistern well is presently equipped with a hand-operated water pump.

In the courtyard behind the church grows a trailing wild raspberry bush, believed to be a descendant of the original Burning Bush. This plant does not produce fruit, but small yellow flowers bloom in season.

A descendant of the Burning Bush, this trailing wild raspberry bush produces a small yellow flower in season.

THE OLD TRAPEZA

During the Frankish rule of Syria, the Crusaders founded the Knights of Sinai for the protection and financial assistance of the monastery. The Old Trapeza, located along the southwest wall, is

The Old Trapeza's walls are decorated with carvings by knights and a large fresco of the Last Judgment.

decorated with many inscriptions which attest to the great number of knights who visited the monastery during the Crusades. Some of these inscriptions are quite elaborate and include a cross, a coat of arms, or the knight's weapons. The oblong hall with pointed Gothic arches houses a large fresco of the Last Judgment, an icon of the Hospitality of Abraham, and a 17th-century carved, wooden table.

THE MONASTERY LIBRARIES

Housed in the concrete building along the southwest wall, which also contains the monks' cells, the **new library** holds the monastery's collection of about 4,500 manuscripts and historical documents, as well as a considerable number of old printed books. The manuscripts are primarily Greek or bilingual Greek and Arabic, but the many in Arabic, Syriac, Georgian, Slavic and Latin testify to the cultural diversity of the brotherhood over the centuries. Many of the texts are illuminated with detailed miniatures. Access to the manuscripts is limited, as there have been thefts of these irreplaceable treasures. The *Codex Sinaiticus*, one of the oldest and most complete Bible manuscripts dating from the 4th century, was stolen by a visiting scholar and presented as a gift to the Russian Tsar. In 1933, the Soviets sold the manuscript to the British Museum where it is now on display. The monastery owns another ancient Biblical manuscript, the *Codex Syriacus*, which dates from the 5th century.

The **old library** now houses a large portion of the monastery's icon collection on the shelves that formerly held books. A selection of the monastery's best icons is presently exhibited in a special room labelled "Picture Gallery" next to the new library, as the majority of visitors are no longer pilgrims coming to venerate the icons, but tourists interested in viewing them as works of art.

THE BONE ROOM

The monastery cemetery with its chapel to St. Tryphon holds only a few graves due to the difficulty of digging graves in the rocky terrain. Monks are buried in the cemetery and later exhumed; their bones are divided and placed among those of their predecessors in the Bone Room. This practice is common in desert monasteries, just as it is on Mount Athos, and serves to remind both monastics and visitors of their inescapable death.

The chronicles of the monastery contain many accounts of righteous fathers whose names have not been preserved. One such account relates that the son of the Emperor Maurice was saved by his nurse when his entire family was killed in a *coup d'etat*. When he came of age and learned his true identity, he left the world and struggled here in humility and asceticism. A few days after his repose, the monks opened his grave and found that his holy relics had been translated. Only decades ago the monks discovered that one of the bones in the pile was exuding myrrh. They reverently placed it in one of the small niches in the wall along with other bones that have been set apart for various reasons.

The Bone Room with the incorrupt relics of St. Stephanos, seated and robed in monastic habit. The skulls of the brethren are behind him.

In the wooden case in the center of the room, the incorrupt relics of St. Stephanos are seated, robed as a monk with a schema and prayer ropes. He lived as a hermit in the 5th century in a cave on the mountain (*The Ladder*, 7:50). During the day he sat at the arch now called **St. Stephen's Gate**, hearing the confessions of those who wished to ascend to the summit. Because the mountain was held in such reverence, anyone who was under an epitemia, or had committed a serious sin, would not be allowed to ascend. St. Stephanos sat at the gate for many decades, and now has been sitting in the Bone Room for 1,400 years, waiting with the brethren for the common resurrection.

Places of Pilgrimage Outside the Monastery

Of the hundreds of chapels in the area, only a few of the more accessible and popular ones will be mentioned. If pilgrims wish, the monastery can arrange for them to be accompanied by a guide.

THE MOUNTAIN PEAKS

Exodus 24:12-18

And the Lord said unto Moses, Come up to Me in the mount, and be there: and I will give thee tables of stone, and a law, and commandments which I have written; that thou mayest teach them. And Moses rose up, and his minister Joshua: and Moses went up into the mount of God... and a cloud covered the mount. And the glory of the Lord abode upon mount Sinai, and the cloud covered it six days: and the seventh day He called unto Moses out of the midst of the cloud. And the sight of the glory of the Lord was like devouring fire on the top of the mount in the eyes of the children of Israel. And Moses went into the midst of the cloud, and gat him up into the mount: and Moses was in the mount forty days and forty nights.

To the south of the monastery, **Mount Sinai** (Jebel Musa) rises 7,500 feet (2,286 m) above sea level. Those wishing to ascend usually follow the path which begins on the eastern side of the monastery. It takes approximately two and a half to three hours to climb to the summit. A chapel was erected at the summit in 363, and rebuilt on a larger scale by Justinian in 527. In 1934 a chapel dedicated to The Most High God was built on a portion of the remaining Justinian foundation with materials from Justinian's chapel. To the left of the chapel, now protected from vandals by a fence, is the **Cleft of the Rock** where God put Moses when he was allowed to see His back parts. A mosque has also been constructed nearby.

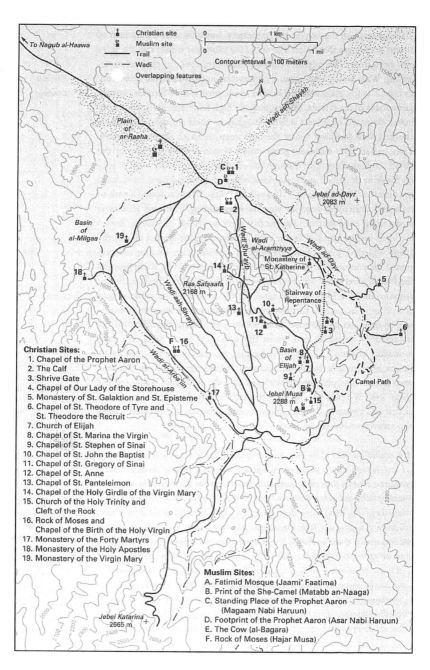

Map of Holy Sites Around Mount Sinai

Reprinted from MOUNT SINAI *by Joseph J. Hobbs, ©1995.*
Courtesy of the University of Texas Press

Exodus 33:18-23

And Moses said, I beseech Thee, shew me Thy glory. And He said, I will make all my goodness pass before thee, and I will proclaim the name of the Lord before thee; and will be gracious to whom I will be gracious, and will shew mercy on whom I will shew mercy. And he said, Thou canst not see My face: for there shall no man see Me, and live. And the Lord said, Behold, there is a place by Me, and thou shalt stand upon a rock: and it shall come to pass, while My glory passeth by, that I will put thee in a clift of the rock, and will cover thee with My hand while I pass by: and I will take away Mine hand, and thou shalt see My back parts: but My face shall not be seen.

Many pilgrims begin their ascent in the early hours of the morning in order to be at the top of the mountain for the exceptional sunrise. The view is one of the most awe-inspiring in the world, as only another pilgrim can attest. To the southwest, the highest

Chapel at the summit of Mt. Sinai dedicated to The Most High God.

mountain in the Sinai Peninsula, **Mount St. Catherine** (Jebel Katerina), rises to a height of 8,650 feet (2,637 m) above sea level. It was to the summit of this mountain that the Angels transported the

Saint's body after her martyrdom. A small white chapel can be seen from the summit of Mount Sinai. Warm clothing is essential for any mountain hike as the temperature drops because of the altitude.

The descent from Mount Sinai is usually via the flight of 3,700 steps to the monastery's south side. One must use caution when descending, since loose gravel can make the stairs slippery. Below the summit is **Mount Horeb**, a plateau with a group of cypress trees (one of which is very old), a well, and several small structures. Some sources state that this is the place where the Seventy Elders of Israel waited for Moses after God called them to worship Him on the mountain (Exodus 24).

Cave of the Prophet Elias on Mount Horeb where he heard the voice of the Lord in a gentle breeze. This cave has been incorporated into the larger church dedicated to the Prophet Elisseus.

The largest of the buildings contains two chapels, one dedicated to the Prophet Elisseus (at the entrance) and one to the Prophet Elias (on the right). In the altar area of the chapel of the Prophet Elias is the small cave where Elias heard the voice of the Lord in a gentle breeze (I Kings 19:9-18). Although it is usually locked, this double chapel may be glimpsed through the large keyhole.

I Kings 19:9-18

And he came thither unto a cave, and lodged there; and, behold, the word of the Lord came to him, and He said unto him, What doest thou here, Elias? And he said, I have been very jealous for the Lord God of hosts: for the children of Israel have forsaken Thy covenant, thrown down Thine altars, and slain Thy prophets with the sword; and I, even I only, am left; and they seek my life, to take it away. And He said, Go forth, and stand upon the mount before the Lord. And, behold, the Lord passed by, and a great and strong wind rent the mountains, and brake in pieces the rocks before the Lord; but the Lord was not in the wind: and after the wind was an earthquake; but the Lord was not in the earthquake: and after the earthquake a fire; but the Lord was not in the fire: and after the fire a still small voice. And it was so, when Elias heard it, that he wrapped his face in his mantle, and went out, and stood in the entering in of the cave. And behold, there came a voice unto him, and said, What doest thou here, Elias? And he said, I have been very jealous for the Lord God of hosts: because the children of Israel have forsaken Thy covenant, thrown down Thine altars, and slain Thy prophets with the sword; and I, even I only, am left; and they seek my life, to take it away. And the Lord said unto him, Go, return on thy way to the wilderness of Damascus: and when thou comest, anoint Hazael to be king over Syria: and Jehu the son of Nimshi shalt thou anoint to be king over Israel: and Elisseus the son of Shaphat of Abel-meholah shalt thou anoint to be prophet in thy room... Yet I have left me seven thousand in Israel, all the knees which have not bowed unto Baal, and every mouth which hath not kissed him.

✠

Dismissal Troparion of the Holy Prophets Elias & Elisseus
Fourth Tone

The incarnate Angel, the summit of the Prophets, the second Forerunner of the coming of Christ, Elias the glorious from on high did send down grace to Elisseus; he driveth away diseases and cleanseth lepers. Wherefore he poureth forth healings upon them that honour him.

✠

St. Stephen's Gate, named for St. Stephanos who heard the confessions of those wishing to ascend to the summit of Mount Sinai. The mountain was held in such reverence that one who had committed a serious sin was not permitted to go further.

If one follows the path down the mountain, the next structure of interest one reaches is **St. Stephen's Gate**, an arch set between two sheer rock cliffs. (For further explanation, please see **The Bone Room**, p.153.)

A short distance from the base of the mountain, located on the path, is a whitewashed chapel dedicated to the Mother of God. Across from it, one can see the watermark made by a spring, now dry, called the **Holy Spring of the Cobbler**. Late in the 15th century (1486), because of the slanderous accusations of a certain Jewish physician, the Patriarch of Alexandria, Joachim, was summoned to an inquest by the Sultan. After a lengthy debate on the Faith, the Patriarch was commanded to prove the validity of his words by moving a mountain near Cairo. He requested a period of several days and sent an encyclical letter asking all the Christians to fast, pray, and entreat God to work a sign. At the appointed time, the Patriarch and a great multitude of people assembled. After praying, the Patriarch commanded the mountain to move. To the terror of everyone present, the mountain obeyed. Feeling himself unworthy of such a miracle, the Patriarch prayed again and it was revealed that the wonder had occurred through the prayers of a certain cobbler. Searching out the cobbler, he questioned him about his way of life. After this, to escape the praise of men, the cobbler fled to Mount Sinai and lived in the aforementioned small chapel. Through his prayers, the spring came forth, supplying him and passersby with water.

Whitewashed chapel of the Mother of God on the path down Mount Sinai.

Those wishing to make the five-hour trip to the chapel on the summit of **Mount St. Catherine** should inquire at the monastery. The chapel is constructed of local irregular granite and mortar which makes it appear white from a distance. Because of the strong winds at this great altitude, the roof is weighed down with rocks. The simply-adorned chapel incorporates the outcropping of the rock on which the relics of St. Catherine were found. On a clear day the two gulfs, Suez and Aqabah, are visible, as well as the mountains of Africa to the west and Saudi Arabia to the east. A modest guest room is also available for those wishing to stay overnight.

To the north of the monastery is **Mount Episteme**, and near its summit is the recently restored hermitage of Sts. Episteme and Galaction.

MOSES' ROCK

Exodus 17:1-6
And all the congregation of the children of Israel journeyed from the wilderness of Sin, after their journeys, according to the commandments of the Lord, and pitched in the wilderness of Rephidim: and there was no water for the people to drink. Wherefore, the people did chide with Moses, and said, Give us water that we may drink. And Moses said unto them, Wherefore chide ye with me? Wherefore do ye tempt the Lord? And the people thirsted there for water; and the people murmured against Moses, and said, Wherefore is this that thou hast brought us out of Egypt, to kill us and our children and our cattle with thirst? And Moses cried unto the Lord, saying, What shall I do unto this people? they be almost ready to stone me. And the Lord said unto Moses, Go on before the people, and take with thee the elders of Israel; and thy rod, wherewith thou smotest the river, take in thine hand, and go. Behold, I will stand before thee there upon the rock in Horeb: and thou shalt smite the rock, and there shall come water out of it, that the people may drink. And Moses did so in the sight of the elders of Israel.

For those who do not have the physical ability to climb Mount Sinai, the less strenuous trip to Moses' Rock can be equally rewarding.

Around the base of Mount Horeb (to the left from the monastery), is the rock that Moses struck twice when Israel was complaining of thirst (Exodus 17:1-7). There are twelve gashes in the rock from which twelve streams of water flowed, one for each of the tribes of Israel. A chapel surrounded by a wall has recently been built at the site. A source of water has been found underneath the area and directed for the needs of the monastery.

☩

Dismissal Troparion of the Holy Prophet Moses
Fourth Tone

By Thy manifestation in the fire and Thine appearance in the flesh, Thou didst make glorious the countenance of Moses. And by Aaron's priesthood according to the Law, Thou didst show forth the figure of the new dispensation of grace: By the prayers of Thy holy Prophets, O Christ God, save our souls.

☩

THOLA

Some five miles from the monastery is Thola, the site of the cave in which St. John Climacus (the author of *The Ladder of Divine Ascent*) struggled for forty years. St. John came to the monastery at the age of sixteen. Although well educated, he submitted to the abbot in all things, embraced silence and humility, and defeated the passions. After nineteen years of cenobitic life, the Saint's elder reposed and the Saint withdrew to this cave in the desert to live in solitude.

Very little is known about his struggles in these years, yet from his known virtues, writings, and miracles, much may be inferred. Once, St. John was in a light sleep in this cave when he received a rebuke from a holy person, "John, how can you heedlessly sleep, when Moses is in danger?" Rising at once, he began to pray for his disciple Moses, whom he had sent on an errand. When the disciple returned, he related that he had been saved from being crushed by a large rock while he was napping at noonday, because he thought he had heard St. John calling him (*The Ladder*, p. xxxvii).

When St. John was made abbot of the monastery, a large crowd of pilgrims gathered. During trapeza St. John saw a man, dressed in a white tunic according to ancient Jewish custom, authoritatively giving orders to the brethren and servants. When they looked for him, St. John informed them that it had been the Prophet Moses. On another occasion, Palestine was saved from a drought by his prayers.

St. John reposed in the first decade of the 7th century at the age of eighty. A modern chapel dedicated to the Saint has been built near his cave.

The cave of St. John Climacus where he spent forty years in harsh asceticism is some five miles from the monastery in a region called Thola.

✠

Dismissal Troparion of St. John Climacus
Third Tone

Having raised up a sacred ladder by thy words, thou wast shown forth unto all as a teacher of monastics; and thou dost lead us, O John, from the purification that cometh through godly discipline unto the light of Divine Vision. O righteous Father, do thou entreat Christ God that we be granted great mercy.

✠

Epilogue

It is hoped that after visiting the numerous holy places around Jerusalem and Mount Sinai, the pilgrim was able to find the stillness and solitude that give wings to prayer. Perhaps to remind pilgrims of this prayerful state, or because of the great love that Christians have for the Holy Land, it was an ancient custom for pilgrims to add the word "pilgrim" to their name after they had returned from Jerusalem. The masculine Greek form is "–, *proskinitís*." In Turkish or Arabic-speaking Christian areas, such as Asia Minor, the word "*Hadji–*" was added as a prefix. In English, "–, palmer" meant pilgrim, denoting the palm staffs which the pilgrim used on the roads to the holy sites and carried home as a blessing. The modern equivalent is the suffix "–, pilgrim."

After making the journey which all Orthodox believers hope to undertake, and toward which they strive, pilgrims findthat Jerusalem never leaves them, even though they might be hundreds or thousands of miles away. One need only hear the hymns from a feast of the Church to be transported back to a particular shrine. One need only see a picture or an icon, or hear a Gospel reading to be venerating once again at the site. And when one rereads his pilgrimage journal, or this little guide book, it's like coming home.

Welcome home, Pilgrim.

Selecteo Bibliography

Avigad, N. "Samaria." In *Encyclopedia of Archaeological Excavations in the Holy Land*, vol. 4. New Jersey: Prentice Hall, Inc., 1978, pp. 1032-1050.

Bernstein, Burton. *Sinai: The Great and Terrible Wilderness*. New York: Viking Press, 1979.

Climacus, St. John. *The Ladder of Divine Ascent*. Trans. by Holy Transfiguration Monastery. USA: HTM, 1979.

Connolly, Peter. *Living in the Time of Jesus of Nazareth*. Israel: Steimatzky Ltd., 1983.

Finegan, Jack. *The Archaeology of the New Testament – The Life of Jesus and the Beginning of the Early Church*. Revised Edition. Princeton: Princeton University Press, 1992.

Forsyth, George H. "Island of Faith in the Sinai Desert." *National Geographic*. vol.125, no.1, (1964), pp. 82-103.

Gafni, Shlomo S. and A. van der Heyden. *The Glory of Jerusalem*. Belgium: Cambridge University Press, 1982.

_____. *The Glory of the Holy Land*. Belgium: Cambridge University Press, 1982.

Galey, John. *Sinai and the Monastery of St. Catherine*. Israel: Massada Publishing Ltd., 1980.

Graham, Steven. *A Tramp's Sketches*. London: MacMillan and Co., Ltd., 1913.

_____. *With the Russian Pilgrims to Jerusalem*. London: MacMillan and Co., Ltd., 1914.

Hoade, Eugene, OFM. *Guide to the Holy Land*. Jerusalem: Franciscan Printing Press, 1983.

Hollis, Christopher and Ronald Browning. *Holy Places*. USA: Frederick A. Praeger, Inc., 1969.

Kamil, Jill. *The Monastery of St. Catherine in Sinai, History and Guide*. Egypt: American University in Cairo Press, 1992.

Kazhdan, Alexander P., Editor-in-chief. *The Oxford Dictionary of Byzantium*. New York: Oxford University Press, 1991.

The Life and Sufferings of St. Catherine the Great Martyr. Trans. by Leonidas Papadopoulos and Georgia Lizardos. Seattle: St. Nectarios Press, 1985.

The Lives of the Saints of the Holy Land and the Sinai Desert. Holy Apostles Convent. Trans. by Leonidas Papadopoulos. USA: Holy Apostles Convent, 1988.

Kronstadt, St. John of. *My Life in Christ.* Jordanville, NY: Monastery of the Holy Trinity, 1984.

Mackowski, Richard S.J. *Jerusalem, City of Jesus.* Grand Rapids: William B. Eerdmans Publishing Co., 1980.

Mar Savva, The Fathers of. *The Monastery of Saint Savva the Sanctified: An Introduction to the Monastery and its Saints.* Jerusalem, 1989.

Monaxi, Taicia. *The Mount of Olives Convent 1886-1986.*

Schaick, Z. *The Sea of Galilee.* Israel: Palphot, Ltd.

Tzaferis, E. *The Monastery of St. Catherine on Mount Sinai.* Greece: Hiera Moni Sina—E. Tzaferis S. A., 1985.

Tzaferis, Vassilios Ph.D. *Holy Land.* Greece: E. Tzaferis S. A., 1987.

_____. *The Monastery of the Holy Cross in Jerusalem.* Greece: E. Tzaferis S.A., 1987.

Velimirovic, Bishop Nikolai. *The Prologue from Ochrid.* Trans. by Mother Maria. Birmingham, England: Lazarica Press, 1986.

Weitzmann, Kurt. *The Monastery of Saint Catherine at Mount Sinai: The Icons, from the 6th to the 10th Century.* Princeton University Press, 1976.

Wilkinson, John. *Egeria's Travels to the Holy Land.* Jerusalem: Ariel Publishing House, 1981. (See also: Same title, London: SPCK, 1973.)

Suggested Reading List

New Testament
Psalter
Old Testament

Account of the Dormition of the Mother of God. A good source is:
   The Life of the Virgin Mary, The Theotokos, by Holy Apostles
   Convent, 1989.

Lives of Saints:
   Abridged lives may be found in several collections of lives of Saints,
   including:
   Great Collection of the Lives of the Saints, Chrysostom Press
   Lives of Saints for Young People, Synaxis Press
   Poulos, *Orthodox Saints,* Holy Cross Press
   The Prologue from Ochrid, Lazarica Press
   Saints for All Ages, Dept. of Religious Eduction, OCA

   Complete lives may be found in:
   The Lives of the Saints of the Holy Land and the Sinai Desert, Holy
   Apostles Convent, 1988.

* Mar Savva, The Fathers of. *The Monastery of Saint Savva the
   Sanctified: An Introduction to the Monastery and its Saints.*
   Jerusalem, 1989.

   St. Catherine: *Sufferings of the Great Martyr Catherine,*
   St. Nectarios Press, 1985.

   St. Cyril of Scythopoulos: *The Lives of the Monks of Palestine,*
   Cistercian Publications, 1991.

   St. George: *The Passion and Miracles of the Great Martyr and
   Victorious Wonderworker, St. George,* St. Nectarios Press, 1988.

   St. Gerasimus of the Jordan: *Orthodox Life,* #2, 1980.

   St. Mary of Egypt: *Life of Our Holy Mother Mary of Egypt,*
   St. Nectarios Press, 1989.

St. Pelagia: *The Lives of the Spiritual Mothers*, Holy Apostles Convent, 1991.

St. Sabbas: *The Life of St. Sava the Sanctified*, Christ the Saviour Church, 1985.

St. Theodosius
Sts. Constantine and Helen } See Collections above
St. Hariton

St. John the Romanian: *Orthodox Life*. vol. 35 #5, Sept-Oct 1984, pp. 16-30 and vol. 30 #6, Nov-Dec 1980, pp. 14-20.

Grand Duchess Elizabeth: Millar, *Grand Duchess Elizabeth of Russia*, Nikodemos Publication Society, 1991.

Other References:

Chitty, Derwas J. *The Desert a City*, SVS Press, 1995.

Egeria: Diary of a Pilgrimage, (Ancient Christian Writers, Vol. 38) Newman Press, 1970.

Geva, Hillel. *Ancient Jerusalem Revealed*, Biblical Archeology Society, 1994.

Knopf Guides: The Holy Land, Alfred A. Knopf, 1995.

Tsafrir, Yoram. *Ancient Churches Revealed*, Biblical Archeology Society, 1993.

"In Memory of Abbot Ignaty of Hebron," *Orthodox Life*, vol. 36 #1, Jan-Feb 1986, pp. 37-39.

Homilies by Mar Jacob, Bishop of Serugh found in *The True Vine*.

Items on Suggested Reading List, except those with *
are available from
ST. NECTARIOS PRESS

1-800-643-4233　(206) 522-4471　*Orders@orthodoxpress.org*
Free catalog available upon request

Glossary

Anchorite – A monastic who lives in seclusion.

Archimandrite – The superior of a monastery or group of monasteries, usually invested with the rank of priest.

Basilica – A building whose main features are: rectangular shape, a nave with aisles, and an apse in the eastern wall.

Caliph – A title denoting a successor of Muhammad as temporal and spiritual head of Islam.

Catholicon – The main church of a monastery.

Cenobitic/cenobium/cenobiarch – A type of monasticism in which a group of monks live a communal life under an abbot. The monks do not have any private possessions. A cenobiarch is the head of a cenobium or group of cenobia.

Compline – Literally, "after supper." The second of the evening services in the daily cycle of services.

Epitemia – A rule of penance assigned by a spiritual father to a penitent. It is given not as a punishment, but for the correction of sin and for the healing of the effects of sin.

Faience – A type of earthenware decorated with opaque, colored glazes.

Firkin – British unit of capacity, usually equal to 1/4 of a barrel.

Hesychast – A monastic who has taken a vow of silence; often one who practices the Jesus Prayer.

Lavra – A form of monasticism in which anchorites living apart from each other have some central organization to provide the weekend services for which the anchorites assemble. In Russia, however, lavras are large cenobitic monasteries.

Metochion – A church or property belonging to a monastery, but in a different location.

Narthex – A vestibule at the west end of the church.

Pantocrator – Literally, "Ruler of All." In icons, a specific pose of our Saviour where He is depicted holding the closed Gospel in His hand. This pose is most commonly seen in the domes of churches.

Protomartyr – Literally, "first martyr." St. Stephen is regarded as the first to be martyred for Christ. St. Thecla is also given this title, being the first woman to contend for our Saviour.

Schema – A piece of material decorated with a cross and many inscriptions, worn by monastics tonsured into the highest state of monasticism.

Trapeza – Literally, "table." The place where food is served in a monastery, as well as the meal itself.

Items that Previous Pilgrims Recommend for a Trip to the Holy Land

IN YOUR CARRY-ON :

Camera, flash, extra batteries, film.

Video camera, tapes, batteries, recharger, adaptor for Israeli electricity.

Medications needed in the next 48 hours.

Hetona* – if you wish to immerse yourself in the Jordan River. Also, a swim suit or some garment to wear under the hetona into the River (most hetonas become see-through when wet). Hetonas should be drip-dried completely. If it is necessary to wash them, they should be treated as holy laundry: they should be hand-washed separately and the water should be poured in a place where it will not be stepped on.

Spending Money – Unless you are planning an expensive purchase, most things can be bought with small bills. Older and worn-looking money is not accepted by most foreign banks, and could cause a problem for storekeepers. Traveller's checks and credit cards are accepted in major areas.

Passport – The U.S. Government suggests that travellers make two photocopies of their passport, leaving one in the U.S. with someone who can be contacted in case of an emergency, and taking the other with them, but keeping it separate from their passport. If you do not have a U.S. passport, contact your travel agent for further information on visas.

These items are lightweight and not easily replaced if your luggage is lost or delayed.

PILGRIMAGE ITEMS:

Items to bless – Icon buttons,* prayer ropes*, Bibles, icons, wedding crowns, etc.

Small ziplock bags, bottles, a large syringe or eyedropper, tape, labels, markers, etc. – if you wish to collect rocks, soil, or oil from the oil lamps at the shrines. Olive oil is also appreciated as a donation or offering at the shrines.

Large towels and a large garbage bag for your wet hetona, undergarment, and wet towels – if you are going to immerse yourself in the Jordan River.

Prayer books, hymns, or services associated with the sites you will be visiting.

Candles are usually available at the shrines, but some pilgrims prefer to bring their own. Also, some pilgrims bring beeswax candles to the shrines as a donation or offering.*

TOILETRY ITEMS:

Soap, shampoo, comb/brush, baby powder, toothbrush, toothpaste, toilet paper (it is good to carry some with you at all times, as the public facilities are usually out), paper toilet seat covers, facial tissue travel packs, handiwipes or baby wipes, ear plugs.

Some medicines to consider: Whatever you normally take for: headache, upset stomach, diarrhea, constipation and allergic reactions. Also consider taking: rub for sore/stiff muscles, insect bite lotion, adhesive bandages, ace bandage, sunscreen and/or lotion for sunburn, etc. There are pharmacies in Jerusalem, but it is better to not spend the time looking for them and the product you need.

CLOTHING:

You are going to the holiest places in the world and will be continually entering churches and shrines.

Women should wear: Modest, comfortable skirts or dresses that come below the knee and up to the neck. Their arms and heads should be covered.

Men should wear: Pants and long-sleeved shirts.

Comfortable walking shoes (preferably with rubber soles), an extra pair of walking shoes, sunglasses, sun hat, sweater or sweatshirt (for early morning and late night), compact umbrella or folding hooded raincoat (during some months it has been known to rain every day), padded hiking socks may be helpful.

Gloves, scarf, hat, warm coat or heavy sweatshirt, flashlight – if you are going to climb Mt. Sinai.

The climate changes with the time of year. Your travel agent will be able to advise you of the average daily weather for your location and month of travel.

MISCELLANEOUS:

Travel alarm clock

Hair dryer (with needed adaptor for Israeli electricity)

Laundry soap – a small bottle for emergencies (hair dryer doubles as clothes dryer).

Water bottle or canteen – most pilgrims prefer not to take the chance of getting sick and drink only bottled water which is readily available.

Waist pack or back pack – as in all congested cities, the Old City of Jerusalem is a favorite place for pickpockets. It is advisable to keep your purse, bags, packs, etc. in front of you, especially during the "rush hour" when pedestrian traffic becomes a pushing mob.

Pens, pencils

Notebook or journal – when conscientiously written, it becomes invaluable when you wish to relive your Holy Land experience.

Travel cup

Snacks and food – for when you need "something" and don't have the time or desire to try the local food. If you plan to visit Mt. Sinai, you must bring your own food.

Walking stick – if you find it helpful for climbing.

Travel pillow – if you are doing a lot of travelling within the Holy Land.

Map – *A Pilgrim's Map of the Holy Land for Biblical Research* may be available in some shops in Jerusalem. It is worth buying for the wealth of information it contains, particularly about Old Testament sites.

Bus Schedule – For those who wish to use public transportation, it would be advisable to obtain a bus schedule, especially in order to know when the buses stop running for the Jewish Sabbath.

* These items can be purchased from Holy Nativity Convent, Brookline, MA. For a catalog, call (617) 566-0156.